YOUR MARKETING PROGRAM AUDIT©

100 Thought-Provoking Self-Appraisal Questions Designed to Improve Your Marketing Program by Building on Strengths and Eliminating Weaknesses

Hal Goetsch

Published by

Business Marketing Association

For information on the Business Marketing Association's programs and publications for business marketing professionals, contact:

Business Marketing Association
150 N. Wacker Drive - Suite 1760
Chicago, IL 60606

800-664-4BMA
www.marketing.org

II

First Edition 1997

Library of Congress Cataloging-in-Publication Data

Goetsch, Hal W.
    Your Marketing Program Audit
    1.Marketing Planning; 2. Marketing
        Management

ISBN 0-9656965-0-2 (Paperbound)
LCCN 96-095040
Copyright TXu 732-051

About the Author

Hal Goetsch is a management consultant, author, and lecturer who specializes in integrated marketing and profit planning for businesses. Goetsch's diversified career spans many years, during which he has held top management positions with both large and small companies engaged in manufacturing, business services, wholesaling, and retailing. A frequent speaker and leader of seminars on business and marketing issues, he has held leadership positions in national trade and professional associations.

Goetsch's academic background includes a business degree from the University of Wisconsin-Whitewater and extensive graduate study at the University of Wisconsin-Madison. He is also a graduate of Northwestern University's Institute for Management, Graduate School of Management. He authored *Developing, Implementing, & Managing An Effective Marketing Plan*, 250 pages, co-published in 1993 by The American Marketing Association and NTC Contemporary Business Books, a Division of NTC Publishing Group, Lincolnwood, Illinois, and many of his articles have appeared in marketing publications.

Dedication

This guidebook is for all my readers who want to strengthen their marketing program — to turn it around, or improve it for better results and greater profitability.

Hal Goetsch

ENDORSEMENT

About 18 years ago, while attending a trade association seminar, I heard a lecture by Hal Goetsch addressing his basic principles of marketing, which have since been used in his books.

Engaging Hal Goetsch as a marketing consultant 18 years ago, and applying his methodology to my embryonic concepts for the emerging "Home & Small Office" consumer, led to a phenomenal explosion of sales and profits. A marketing plan was designed to address the needs of these convenience-seeking and price-conscious consumers searching for office supplies at mass market retailers. ACCO World Corporation, a division of American Brands—a Fortune 100 company, later experienced sales increases from one million per year, to over two hundred million dollars per year.

Without a doubt, Hal's marketing principles were fundamentally responsible for ACCO's success with mass market retailers, and my becoming Vice President, Retail Division of ACCO. This led to my next successful venture.

As a busy consultant, application of Hal's latest book, YOUR MARKETING PROGRAM AUDIT, is the best method I know for determining, in a relatively short period, if a company should consider expenditures related to complete development of a major project. Serious, objective application of YOUR MARKETING PROGRAM AUDIT, and applying honest quantitative numerical assessment of the audit's basic factors, will result in the best assessment possible of the product, or idea, being considered. When Hal's marketing audit program process results in positive numbers, the ensuing creation of a complete marketing plan has been simplified; and it has a very high probability of success.

Accountants use audits, and now the marketing world has a valuable YOUR MARKETING PROGRAM AUDIT. Many thanks to Hal Goetsch for its development, and allowing me to use his concept so successfully.

Don Peterson, President, Marketing and Sales Services
1970 Cranbrook Road - Green Oaks, IL 60048-1505

AUTHOR'S PREFACE

Back in 1979, when I wrote my first book about preparing and implementing marketing plans, I likened marketing planning to apple pie and motherhood. That's because most people espoused marketing plans, but not very many actually prepared and used them successfully.

After 17 years, the picture hasn't changed. Far too many, both large and small, for-profit or non-profit businesses of all descriptions, still view "marketing" primarily as selling. Rarely do their descriptions include all the activities that are part of the marketing function. Marketing, for many, is still an esoteric word. Some of the reasons for misunderstandings about marketing's role in our business environment will be discussed as I write about implementing **YOUR MARKETING PROGRAM AUDIT©**.

Some managers, marketing academics, and business writers have coined new buzzwords to describe our current marketing world. Descriptions like customer focused, relationship marketing, integrated marketing, team marketing, total quality marketing, down sizing, up sizing, and real sizing are but a few more popular ones. They sound good, but none of them reflect the correct organizational structure, or the action, required to accurately accomplish this verbiology. Impressive as these buzzwords sound, they're meaningless without company framework and subsequent action that will make these "feeling good" definitions a reality.

Roger S. Peterson, business writer and consultant, aptly describes our current picture. He says: *"American companies are running so fast, they rarely take time to ask themselves basic questions: "What do we really sell?" "What is our singular best advantage over our competitors?" "What would 10 percent of our customers really say about us?" "This is the stuff of strategic planning and it begins with a complete marketing audit."*

Peterson goes on to say: *"Americans smirk when they see Japanese managers stamp their approval on company plans. It's not parts or widgets they're approving. They're building consensus on strategy, tactics, and mission, too. American companies misuse and underuse marketing, because they don't do formal audits of their marketplace assumptions. Most Americans walk down the sidewalks of Enterprise Lane, stepping in all the puddles, and wondering why their shoes are wet. Had they planned their walk by revisiting all their assumptions about the neighborhood, and arrived at consensus about their destination, they wouldn't have wet feet."*

YOUR MARKETING PROGRAM AUDIT© isn't sophisticated or theoretical. Nor is it pedantic, lacking hands-on experience. You don't need to be a PhD or rocket scientist to easily use my common sense, business-tested audit to properly assess *all* elements of your marketing environment, both *internal* and *external*, as the first critical step for building a solid foundation for your complete marketing plan. From extensive and varied business experience, I've learned that management decisions are usually better resolved if they're studied in management by objective (MBO) fashion by informed problem solvers. Herein lies the *real* value of my guide book about carefully and thoroughly conducting a marketing audit before embarking on your marketing venture. All key personnel, not just the CEO or the marketing group, can come together and analytically evaluate strengths and weaknesses in their marketing situation—emphasizing strengths and minimizing weaknesses—just as a coach readies his team for the competition.

Yes, even non-profit agencies and professional associations can use **YOUR MARKETING PROGRAM AUDIT**© to properly appraise their situation. Non-profit groups tend to shy away from "profit" as an undesirable word for them to use. However, "profit" can also be defined as an advantageous gain or a tangible return to the organization and its membership. For example, membership increases can represent the goal of a non-profit venture. I mention this because I'm frequently asked by non-profit groups for reference sources that can help them prepare their marketing plan. They mistakenly believe their planning needs are different from for-profit groups. Only the semantics vary, because the marketing planning process is essentially the same. In reality, all they need to do is substitute their goal and objectives to achieve it, as *benefits* otherwise expressed in dollars by for-profit groups.

My newest guidebook responds to widespread need for *better* examination of our marketing environment, both external and internal, before we embark on a marketing venture. The *first step* in my 4-step **EPIC**© (Examine, Plan, Implement, and Control) recipe for launching a successful marketing plan starts with a complete, *factual* examination of where we've been, where we want to go, and what we must do to get there. Done hastily or carelessly, the foundation for your marketing house will collapse, unable to withstand the fast-changing climate and the competitive winds it will encounter.

Emphasis given in STEP I—Examine—is shown in the marketing planning calendar (timetable) included in the Appendix, *Exhibit 6*. Note that 30 percent of the 20-week timespan for examining, preparing, implementing, and controlling a plan is devoted to the first step, a thorough examination of your marketplace. The planning calendar sets schedules and deadlines. A timetable spread over four months is not inordinately long, and especially if formal planning is being done for the first time. Research required to gather factual information requires a longer timeframe. Hurried planning always leads to poor, faulty programs. Then, too, longer planning time minimizes disruption to on-going business activity.

Benefits of a planning calendar are in its *objectivity*. In poorly managed cases, planning drifts along into the next fiscal year because concerted effort isn't made to start and stop on time. A well-thought-out calendar avoids last-minute, hasty planning. It encourages everyone to *work together within deadlines*. If done correctly, it's an intricate and time-consuming process. Now if this represents a roadblock, consider the alternatives. Chance and chaos are not a prescription for survival and growth. Conversely, rewards make the task worthwhile and rewarding.

You've heard it all before and perhaps said it yourself. "We're not IBM, Proctor and Gamble, Boeing, or General Motors. We can't even think about, much less take the time necessary to prepare and launch a plan like theirs." The truth is, you can't. You probably don't have to. **YOUR MARKETING PROGRAM AUDIT**© is aimed at businesses of any size, including those with limited budgets and manpower.

My down-to-earth, realistic, time tested approach to preparing your plan, and implementing it *on time*, gives you a roadmap for marketing success. You may not have taken a methodical and calculated approach to formal marketing planning for your product (or service) in the past. You may have used "gut feeling" attempts that produced disappointing results. Or, you may be uncertain about how to proceed. My audit will help you avoid pitfalls, and provide the base for a marketing plan that pays back much more than it costs.

Please feel free to contact me for any assistance you may need to get started. In addition to **YOUR MARKETING PROGRAM AUDIT**©, the Appendix of my guidebook gives you additional assistance for preparing, implementing and controlling your plan.

Hal Goetsch, President
Marketing and Management Services
4151 Marla Drive, NE
Albuquerque, NM 87109-1924
Ph. (505) 889-9418

Contents

XII

Appendix

Exhibit

STEP 1 - EXAM

"If we could first know where we are, and whither we are tending, we could better judge what to do, and how to do it."

....Abraham Lincoln
(Speech to Illinois State Republican Convention, June 17, 1858)

Serious marketing planners can implement Lincoln's words by asking some basic questions to be answered in the audit process. Those questions are as follows:

- Where are we?
- Where do we want to go?
- Can we get there?
- What must we do to get there?

Assessment, or self-examination, helps us get where we want to go. This is the basis of sound decision-making, which requires moving critical resources in the right direction. Doing this necessitates an audit: A complete, annual physical exam of *all* marketing activities to pinpoint opportunities for better action-taking decisions. Like a physician's diagnosis, plans for achieving marketing objectives will result from *thorough self-appraisal*. Sound marketing decisions usually are simple when they come from informed planners.

But even when a conscientious attempt is made to see a situation objectively, the focus can be

blurred by tradition, unquestioned procedures, per-
sonalities, manipulated programs, corporate politics,
indifference, or laziness. Too often, the picture is
faulty because important facts are missing, guesses
are not reliable, or some critical elements of the
picture are ignored or overlooked.

Herein lies the value of the marketing audit. Its
purpose is to generate areas of discussion that
identify *deficiencies* for correction and *strengths* for
exploitation. Many companies make the common
mistake of limiting their options. They do not stand
back and objectively look at what they are accom-
plishing, what their competition is doing, and what
their customers want. They are frequently under
pressure not to rock the boat. Corporate myopia and
atrophy blinds participants to plan "the way it's
always done." Following a precedent is an easy
substitute for thinking. Conversely, careful
examination of *all* marketing components serves to
provide **action** instead of **denial**.

A *thorough* and *complete* audit will provide
insight into performance, pointing to strengths and
weaknesses to be addressed in marketing planning.
Audits are also crucial to the marketing function in
organizations where managerial perceptions often
differ from reality. For these reasons, an increasing
number of companies and other organizations are
regularly conducting audits in their effort to keep
pace with rapidly changing marketing conditions.

Thus, unless marketing plans are built on a sound
FACT BASE, the finished product will be faulty and
subject to failure. That means shortcuts should

never be taken in this critical, *first* planning step. If facts are not readily available, every effort must be made to get them. Out of expedience, "guessimates" assumptions, or carelessness are unacceptable.

Evaluate your company's marketing performance using this point system: Excellent 4, Good 3, Fair 2, Poor 1. Then tally total score for an overall report card of performance: Above 360, Excellent; 279-359, Good; 120-278, Fair; Below 120, Poor. Score a "4" on any question wherein your business, agency, or association doesn't apply and tally total points for your performance appraisal.

Following are some questions to determine if there are roadblocks in your marketing environment (both internal and external), strengths to maximize, and weaknesses to correct.

Corporate Marketing Culture
- Proactive, Customer-Focused Commitment

Studying the marketing environment starts with commitment from the top down. To be marketing-driven and customer-focused requires much more than lip service, especially from the chief executive. The CEO must be the driving force, instilling and implementing marketing plans that take into account every aspect of the marketing environment—the *catalyst* for all other plans—finance, personnel, engineering, inventory, production, etc. In short, *positioning* the marketing plan as the engine of the train, not the caboose!

1. Does the CEO believe in marketing planning as the basis and forerunner of all other business planning, including a business plan? Is a marketing plan used to prepare the other plans? Is your marketing plan the engine for the train, or is it the caboose? _____

2. Is a formal planning process ingrained with all managers in the business? Do they manifest a positive, proactive mindset? Are they involved in the marketing planning process, rather than restricting participation to your marketing group? _____

3. If a written marketing plan exists, is performance regularly measured against it? Are changes made for necessary adjustments during the course of its progress? _____

4. Are marketing plans prepared with full participation of all functional managers, or are they dictated primarily by the CEO or a few key staff? _____

5. Is computer technology being used to build a marketing database, and do managers understand its capabilities? _____

6. Are all marketing functions under the direction of one marketing head who reports to the CEO? Are they inte-grated into one centralized department

and not fragmented? Is your marketing head comparable to that of a quarterback for a football team, a first-level decision maker?   _____

7. Is marketing planning started well ahead of your plan-year's start date to prevent hurried results and to avoid interference with daily work routines? Are schedules (with deadlines) set to prevent last-minute, hurried, or incomplete plans?   _____

8. Do marketing plans include all components of your marketing activity, or are they mainly sales projections and broad market objectives lacking specifics and datelines for completion?   _____

Successful businesses, whether for-profit or non-profit, do not evolve without hard work and good marketing planning, implementation, and control. Those lacking thoroughness and formality in their planning are courting eventual disaster. Chances are good that if a plan can't be put in writing, it really isn't a very good plan. Countless examples in corporate graveyards will attest to this fate.

Granted, formal planning doesn't ensure successful performance, but it does provide disciplined appraisal, goal setting, and action steps to maximize chances for success. Even in our ever-changing environment, written plans will help to determine the best application of resources for their most profitable use. They are an organized thought process, a *communication system*.

Sad to say, even in this age of enlightenment, the great majority of business just don't get it! Only a minority have complete, written marketing plans that are implemented reasonably well. Obstacles can usually be traced directly to attitude and action of the CEO. Many CEOs lack marketing orientation and hands-on experience. Too often, they view marketing only as a "selling" function. Surveys show that fewer than 25 percent of all CEO's career backgrounds include hands-on marketing experience. This is one of the main reasons why most traditional business plans don't lead with a complete marketing plan preceding the rest of their plans. In these cases, marketing isn't the engine pulling the train. Plainly stated, these business plans are not customer-focused or marketing-integrated. They lack inclusion of all marketing components, the *6 P's—people, product, price, promotion, place*, and *profit.*

A model, showing how integrated and marketing-driven businesses should operate, is illustrated in *Exhibit 1*, in the Appendix. In this schematic, a complete marketing plan leads the way for all other plans. The basis for other operating plans, it's positioned up front at the beginning of planning activity. This approach is *proactive* and in sharp contrast to planners who write and talk about being marketing driven and customer focused, but who show little evidence to support these claims in their business plans. Their marketing planning data is sketchy; it usually consists of extrapolations of sales projections that comply with financial goals. Put simply, a complete marketing plan must be prepared as the forerunner of any business plan. When the schematic shown in *Exhibit 1* is followed, a proactive business plan results. A plan which is truly customer-focused and marketing integrated!

The **EPIC**© planning process is illustrated in *Exhibit 2* in the Appendix. It includes all marketing components, not just the sales department. This process is visualized as a wheel, shown in *Exhibit 3* in the Appendix. The hub is the marketing *goal*, supported with marketing spokes that represent *objectives* which support the hub. *Strategies* and *tasks* required to fulfill objectives constitute the wheel's rim.

Readers who are seriously interested in starting formal marketing planning for their own situations will find helpful planning assistance in *Exhibits 4 through 8*, in the Appendix. These include the following:

- Benefits of marketing planning;
- Marketing planning pitfalls;
- Calendar for marketing planning;
- Criteria for a good marketing plan; and,
- Guidelines for making people more agreeable to change.

Marketing plans are not mandates; they are *direction*. They do not determine the future, but they are *commitments* to mobilize the resources and energies of the business in order to create the future.

Too often, marketing plans are shortchanged with inadequate preparation time and disregard for their implementation or control and adjustment after they're set in motion. Remember, if done methodically, it's a time-consuming process. If this represents a deterrent, consider the alternatives. Chance and chaos are not a prescription for survival and growth. Nor are they a sign of control and purpose in the management of the business. Conversely, rewards make the task a worthwhile investment.

Products and Services
- Vehicle for Existence

The success of any marketing program starts with a *thorough* knowledge of the product or service offered; their *true value to users*. Critical information must be gathered and evaluated, because it is essential to clearly understand current offerings before making decisions for future marketing activity. Acceptance and use of computers for a database is a necessity, not a convenience. Objectively gather information for evaluation, cooperation, and participation from *all* other areas of the company, not just the marketing department! These are some questions to use for examination:

9. What are the user benefits of your product and service? Are they recognized, and effectively exploited? _____

10. What is their life cycle stage? (introduction, growth, maturity, saturation, decline). Is a continuous program used to weed out unprofitable products or services? Should you add new ones? Rejuvenate or reposition others? Can products be modified to reach other markets? _____

11. Are product/services profiles developed? Are they user-focused? Designed for needs of the user? Do they exploit your key competencies? _____

12. Are inexpensive methods used to estimate new product/service potentials before considerable amounts are spent on development or market introductions? _____

13. Is it customary to first launch new products/services with field tests, forecasts, and pricing before funds are spent on advertising, promotion, and distribution systems? Are these costs calculated and included in marketing plan budgets? _____

14. What percentage of sales/profits came from new products/services in the last three years? Are returns on invested capital for new products/services compared with actual outlays? And forecasts? _____

15. Is new product/services activity characterized as innovative, or is it generally a cosmetic refinement of existing products or services? ____

16. Have trends in new materials, technology, and government regulations been studied each plan year? Are they included in planning assumptions? ____

17. Is product/services safety a "positioning" advantage in your marketplace? Is it emphasized in marketing strategy? ____

18. Are products/services offered in their most appealing and cost-effective way for the markets being served? Are logos and corporate signage used on all products and collaterals? ____

The ultimate goal for any new product or service is to be able to *anticipate* needs of the marketplace. To be proactive, rather than reactive, requires perception of customers needs, whether they're expressed or latent. Marketers should pay more attention to what would-be users do, not just to what they say. The more informed the marketer is about the customer, the greater the opportunity.

At the same time it's important for companies to know what they're best at doing. They must stick to their knitting and be ready to exploit their core skills and resources.

Few companies manage to attain the anticipatory level because their stockholders and leadership are driven to produce short-term profits without incurring additional costs for expensive research and development. They're not willing to risk investment in something that hasn't been specifically requested. It's always easier to be reactive—to follow rather than lead.

Successful anticipatory marketing requisites include the following:

- Understanding customers' needs from the customers' perception;

- Staying close and alert... listening to would-be users;

- Making a continuing investment in innovative research;

- Willingness to develop products or services that haven't been requested;

- Matching new products and services with the right distribution channels; and,

- Supporting introductions with adequate advertising and promotion;

There are few manufacturers that can match 3M's new product leadership. Their annual report for year ending 1995 indicates another record high in sales and profit, new products, global growth, and stockholders' dividends. Twenty-seven percent of net sales ($13,460 billion) came from new products introduced during the last four years. 3M's record of innovation and its reputation as a premier organization were validated again in 1995. They received the national Medal of Technology, the highest award bestowed by the President of the United States for technological achievement, for the many innovations and thousands of successful products 3M has introduced over 90 years. Much of this product success is attributed to having *design, production, and marketing teams* that work more closely in groups. Significantly, their continuous growth focuses on five key strengths: market leadership, technological innovation, customer focus, global reach, and employee initiative. In 1995, international sales in over 200 countries outside the United States were 54 percent of total. They're represented with companies in over 60 countries. 3M has created a risk-taking culture that encourages sharing ideas and know-how and fosters dedication and drive. For example, their scientists are encouraged to spend 15 percent of the time pursuing their own ideas. Whether large or small, more manufacturers need to take lessons from them.

Any new product/service should be fully tested and proved reliable. More often than not, they fail in the marketplace because they weren't de-bugged before they were prematurely rushed to market. Delivery and service reliability are also essential if the product/service is going to be valued in a competitive marketplace. Certainly Maytag's success in the home laundry market is ample testimony to this premise.

A handy checklist for screening any new product/ service is shown in *Exhibit 9* in the Appendix.

Like people and customers, products also have their life cycles: *conception, adolescence, maturity, decline*, and *death*. Products don't last forever. Their length of life depends on many variables influenced by customers, competitors, and many other external and internal factors. Generally representing the shape of a bell-curve, product strategy must be geared to differing conditions prevailing in each stage of the life cycle. Characteristics of each life cycle stage are shown in *Exhibit 10*, in the Appendix. Understanding these characteristics is critical to marketing factors such as pricing, advertising and promotion, target marketing and segmentation, product modification, and new product development.

Matrixation (perceptual planning) is a helpful tool for identifying problems, focusing attention, and transplanting situations into *visual* values for easier comprehension. Graphic presentations make it easier to grasp complex abstractions. They can be used very effectively. For example, *Exhibit 11* depicts product/service profitability in relation to market share. The "3" rating on the vertical scale for profitability, and "8" on the horizontal scale for market share intersect in the "problem" quadrant indicates a need for remedial action.

The Customer - Reason for Existence

Market research must be conducted for something that is not in the market. Defining a potential market for something new requires asking if there is a *need* for what the product or service will do. *Customers define markets*. Their *demographic* (population mix) and *psychographic* (buying motivation) characteristics must be identified to effectively reach them. User profile and satisfaction levels must be determined to respond to *needs* and *wants*. Some important questions include the following:

19. Does everyone from top to bottom regard customers as the most important part of your business? Does everyone know why customers in your markets should do business with you? Why is it beneficial for them? Do they know what user benefits you offer? _____

20. How is customer feedback gathered? Is it focused on what they're really saying? Are they systematically surveyed (at least annually) using Web page, on-line e-mail, fax, or other direct contact methods that factually collect information about their level of satisfaction and needs? _____

21. Does your business respond quickly to orders and service requirements? Is strategy structured to supply information about order status, service inquiries, pricing, and inventory on a

timely basis? Is everyone service minded? _____

22. Who are your major customers? What percent of sales/profits do they really contribute? Is their retention rate acceptable? Do you really know why they leave? Is more effort spent to keep customers than is spent to replace them? _____

23. Is there a national key account program in place? Is it managed with on-line transmission of orders, inventory, service, and marketing information? _____

24. Are account profiles maintained in your account database? Can they be readily accessed for history, profitability, personnel status, locations, inventory, and other necessary information? _____

25. Do all employees, the entire business, know what customer service means in terms of their responsibility and contribution to profits? Is good service viewed as value added? _____

Our information age places profound emphasis on the customer as paramount to success. *Service* is on the front line of the new economy as we approach the 21st Century. Prominent, rapid, crea- tive, and personalized—it is the ultimate strategic imperative. Customers are the boss's boss. Today, the customer is king! Management guru Peter

Drucker, writing earlier in "The Practice of Management," summarized this concept when he wrote: *"There is only one valid definition of business purpose: To create a customer."*

Businesses surviving in our fast-paced, competitive, and ever-changing environment are those which can adapt and innovate according to customers' needs, not sellers' dictates. Size couldn't save the dinosaur. Extinction is inevitable when companies don't change their marketing strategies in the face of losing customers and falling profits. What worked in the past can become a trap. *Inflexibility and contentment results in marketing inertia.*

Yes, customer satisfaction must be the main objective of any business. Studies indicate that, on average, a satisfied customer tells five others, but nine out of ten unhappy ones don't voice their complaints when service is poor. They simply go elsewhere. One unhappy customer has the potential, on average, to badmouth a company to 10 or 15 others. These same findings also show it's five times more expensive to land a new, good customer than it is to keep an old one.

We're greatly concerned about improving customer service, but this effort must start with the practice of *internal marketing*, an idea stemming from the fact that any business or organization is only as good as its people. Most businesses, whether for-profit or non-profit, screen and hire for skills and experience when they should hire for *attitude* and train for skills.

Customer service, being user-focused, must emanate from within. If people producing or selling products or services aren't sold, customers won't be either. Accountants are an essential part of financial services, teachers a crucial part of educational services, ticket agents and stewards present an image of airlines' services, and office receptionists convey tone and attitude of their company. In reality, customers *buy* the *people* when the buy their products or services. If employees don't meet customers' expectations, then neither does the product or service they're representing.

Dissatisfactions of customers indicate where to look for business potential. Converting them from problems into opportunities brings extraordinary gains. Are we really interested in our customer? Test customer rapport with these statements:

- I'm always friendly, helpful and concerned.
- I never judge a customer by their appearance.
- I never interrupt a customer. I let them finish their entire thought.
- I always concentrate on what the customer is saying.
- I always look the customer in the eye.

If we're completely honest, the chances are that we can't answer all of these statements with a "yes".

Growing a business and keeping more customers is a basic tenet for success. Far beyond the rhetoric of being customer-oriented, successful firms have reduced *customer satisfaction* to a practice. Potter Palmer, founder of Marshall Field and Company, revolutionized merchandising when he established the policy of allowing customers to return merchandise. His philosophy, like that of Montgomery Ward who followed him, was that the customer's interest is paramount.

Putting the customer first is a cornerstone for Nordstrom, a Seattle-based specialty chain founded in 1901. They listen to their customers. Another reason for their superior profitability is because their inventory is double that of the industry. They emphasize that a missing item is a missing sale and a disappointed customer. Their average sales per square foot were around $400 in 1995 as compared to Federated's $190 and May Department Stores' $185. Computerized inventory control systems allow buyers and store managers to plan inventories, classify sales by size and color, plan mark downs, and project profits. The system is networked so any buyer can check sales of an item across the chain.

After being recognized as a disaster, IBM has regained the respect of Corporate America. It's nearing double-digit growth for the first time in seven years. Under Gerstner, Big Blue went back to the basics of how to succeed in business by talking to customers, finding out what they need, and satisfying them. From the beginning, Gerstner rebuilt relationships with IBM's largest customers by getting out of the office and meeting regularly with customers. According to his own calculations, he spends 40 percent of his time talking with customers. This contrasts dramatically with IBM's distant, arrogant, and unresponsive attitude before Gerstner's arrival. Now they are organized around marketing units targeted at specific industries such as insurance, banking, healthcare, and education. IBM foresees great growth potential by providing customers with complex software, systems, and networks for electronic commerce.

Companies grow when they put customers **first**, and maintain constant, quality communication with them. Loyal customers keep coming back. Operating costs go down when marketers don't have to spend disproportionate time and effort finding new prospects to replace lost customers. Employee retention improves as pride in serving customers increases. It's axiomatic that satisfied workers encourage people to buy more. Astute marketers target customers carefully, nurture their relationships, and treat employees the way they want them to treat customers.

The French expression *cherchez le creneau*, meaning "look at the hole," is another apt description of important marketing strategy. Studying market segments and customer needs is crucial for any product or service to be successful in our fiercely competitive, fast changing marketplace.

Major trends in buying power, buying behavior, and customer needs can be determined by analyzing what is taking place in population dynamics and structure. Movement to the Sunbelt and Rocky Mountain States, baby booms, education and income level changes, concern for personal safety, employment opportunities, energy conservation, waste recycling, use of leisure time, personal values, inflation—all are social and economic factors requiring careful assessment. Trends toward conservative or liberal lifestyles can create opportunities or present problems. For example, tobacco and liquor industries face severe restrictions because their products are detrimental to health. Firearm manufacturers are barraged with citizens' demands for legislation that can restrict their business.

Too often, market research is confined to existing customers rather than to all users in a market. Most companies don't pay enough attention to those who aren't buying from them. Should-be customers are a critical group to watch, because their wants can be exploited as opportunities.

To illustrate this, mainline churches and synagogues in United States have been losing some members to "new thought" pastoral churches that ask members what they need and want in a church. Their focus is on the individual's spiritual wants and needs, unfettered with religious tradition and dogma. "Should be" customers are a group to watch and exploit, because their wants and needs represent opportunities.

McDonald's family restaurants pioneered the concept of curbside service by identifying a need for fast, quality food service at affordable prices. Jiffy Lube, the earliest and largest lube and oil change franchise, followed suit. Capitalizing on the example of Federal Express courier service, the Japanese identified the need for the fax machine. Instead of asking whether there was a need, they evaluated the *potential* for what the fax machine could do for customers. Ironically, while the machine is an

American invention, few if any are produced in United States.

Psychographics is the cognizance of peoples' attitudes and habits, and is basic to positioning products or services... establishing an identity that differentiates from competitors. Why do people buy? Here are some reasons:

Impulse	Popularity	Necessity
Price	Prestige	Desire
Availability	Value	Tradition

Reasons why people don't buy include:

No need   No money   No hurry
No desire   No trust

Business, for-profit or non-profit, must constantly improve their *profile* from the customer's viewpoint. Factors of consideration, things weighing into people's decision to become a customer, include:

Image & reputation	Special services
Unique selling points	Guarantees
Pricing	Product line/s
Perceived goals	Payment options
Management & staff	Location
Service efficiency	Facilities & appearance

Delivering great customer service keeps customers coming back. Companies that serve us best will continue to get the business! Discerning consumers require *superlative service*.

Markets and Marketing Channels
- Sales Targets and Selling Paths

After profiling the customers, both existing and potential, it becomes necessary to assess the most appropriate *segments* of your total market universe and the selling systems to reach them. This examination reveals strengths and weaknesses in the *customer base* and will also reveal which segments should be targeted. The following questions will stimulate evaluation.

26. Has the market's size and company's share been reliably determined? Are these estimates or facts? _____

27. How is your market universe shaped? Have all segments been identified and measured? Projected for the next 3 - 5 years? _____

28. Which markets are growing and which ones are declining? How are you reacting to these changes? Have you abandoned some and entered others in recent years? Is there on-going research and surveillance to monitor them? Are current (or anticipated) product/services and marketing trends likely to affect us? _____

29. Has the company's vision broadened? Do you explore and evaluate new markets? Do they require product/

service differentiation or different
marketing and distribution systems?   _____

30. Are global opportunities being pursued?
     If not, why not?   _____

31. What percent of total sales/profits
     come from new markets entered in the
     last several years? Is it acceptable?   _____

Estimates of market size are crucial to determine if there is sufficient potential to justify a viable avenue of opportunity. Relying on subjective judgements without a factual base of information is dangerous ground. For example, entrepreneurs, usually sparked with great enthusiasm and vision of success, often fail because they haven't spent enough time studying the market(s) for their product or service. Conversely, their market assessment may be accurate, but the channels of distribution may be ineffective and unprofitable. They may be using a shotgun, spraying pellets over a wide area of coverage in hopes of scoring some hits when a rifle is needed to zero-in on more appropriate targets.

Companies embarking on marketing planning for the first time are apt to face serious shortages of factual information necessary for a thorough audit. Larger firms, or those with financial resources, can retain professional market researchers specializing in their field of interest. Small or financially limited companies may consider the undertaking too time-consuming and too expensive. This erroneous assumption can be corrected if enough time and effort are used to exploit inexpensive sources of information.

Excellent sources of marketing information include trade associations, industry publications, trade shows and conventions, and government agencies. The federal government is a treasure house of mostly free (or inexpensive) information for market research. Used by few other than professional researchers, its resources are available for the asking. For example, the Census Bureau's billion dollar market study has a wealth of data covering retail, wholesale, manu-facturing, and service companies. Some government sources for information include the following:

- The Bureau of the Census and Census Data User's Office is a central contact for more than 100 experts on retail, manufacturing, wholesale, and service company data. The economic census, updated every five years, provides data from a survey of manufacturers and service businesses.

- The Federal Data Procurement Center is a computer database for federal contracts and add-ons of $10,000 plus.

- The Securities and Exchange Commission requires 10-K Corporate filings for all publicly owned companies engaged in interstate commerce.

- The Department of Commerce collects data on any business topic, domestic and overseas.

- The Library of Congress is a national referral center and world's largest research center. It is not a lending library for individuals, but does make material available on inter-library loan basis.

- The United States Government Printing Office publishes the Commerce Department's Statistical Abstract, an annual document of statistics about the population of United States.

Information for establishing markets, staking out sales territories, setting up service centers, and many other important marketing activities such as advertising and promotion should be collected into a data bank by market, company or customer, zip code, six-digit Standard Industrial Classification (SIC) code, size, product, and more. Much of this information is available and defined by the U.S. Government's Office of Management and Budget as Standard Metropolitan Statistical Areas (SMSA), Designated Market Area (DMA), or Area of Dominant Influence (ADI). Computerized street maps of the United States, based on the 1990 Census, can size up neighborhoods by income, age, level of education, number of children, ethnic background, and other characteristics. For a list of firms selling software for these maps, write to the Data User Services Division, Census Bureau, Washington DC 20233.

Any discussion of markets and marketing channels must recognize the omnipresence of cyber power, the birth of *digital commerce* as a critical new lubricant for buyers and sellers of goods and services to communicate with each other. Building blocks for electronic commerce are rapidly falling into place as more people and companies are getting wired, making the Web a business-to-business marketplace.

Can money be made on the Net? Not a lot yet, but scores of entrepreneurs have been quietly experimenting by creating new business models for retailing, marketing, publishing, and advertising that work for them. A survey of 1,100 Web-based businesses, conducted by market researcher ActivMedia, showed that 31 percent claimed to be profitable and 28 percent said they will be in the next two years.

The promise of reaching good prospects, not just consumers who might be in the market, is persuading more major advertisers to invest in Web ads. Toyota runs ads on sites ranging from Parent Soup (parentsoup.com) to ESPNet SportZone (espn.com). Visitors to Toyota's site can order interactive CD-ROMS showing off features of Toyota models, and before the CD-ROM arrives in the mail, a local dealer will call, inviting the Web surfer to come in for a test drive.

Corporate America is discovering that the small business sector represents an untapped market that can be reached as more of the millions of small businesses in the U.S. become wired. Network hardware is easier to buy and set up than ever before. Small business is the third largest economy in the world, after the U.S. and Japan. According to the SBA, the number of companies with fewer than 100 employees has increased nearly 50 percent since the early 1980s. These 20 million small enterprises account for about half the nation's employment and more than 30 percent of gross national product. Networking help from brand-name companies include Microsoft, IBM, Novell, Hewlett-Packard, AT&T, and 3COM. There are an estimated 30,000 consulting firms specializing in networking software... recommending, installing, and servicing entire networks for markets such as legal, medical, retail, etc. Local phone companies have launched installation services, which include Internet access.

The use of on-line databases is growing, but they're still a relatively minor source of information for most business buyers. A recent study conducted by Penton Research Services found that 41.2 percent of business-purchase decision makers have access to on-line databases. The largest share use Internet, followed by CompuServe and America On-Line. Another 32.7 percent expect to use on-line sources of information in the future. While companies are preparing for the future by developing on-line presence, they're continuing to focus marketing efforts on information sources that decision makers rely on most: business magazines, directories, salespeople, and trade shows.

For marketers, *global marketing literacy* is as important as computer literacy. International markets are fraught with problems of language barriers, cultural differences, government regulations, and varying buying patterns. Nevertheless, there's unlimited opportunity. It's a lifeline to the future!

Global screening criteria varies by industry, by product, and service. A useful summary list of criteria follows:

- Goals and strategies
- Size of firm
- Financial strength
- Reputation
- Trading areas covered
- Compatibility
- Experience
- Sales organization
- Physical facilities
- Willingness to carry inventories
- Service capability
- Use of promotion
- Sales performance
- Relations with local government
- Communications
- Overall attitude

To a great extent these characteristics parallel those used to screen domestic distributors, but there are notable exceptions. For example, the intermediary's relationship with government may be of paramount importance, overshadowing all other considerations.

International marketing is the great business adventure of our time. It's competitive, risky, and full of unknowns. But the rewards are great for those who are able to meet the challenges of the global arena.

Sales History - Previous Marketing Results

Records for the past three to five years reveal trends, spot problems, and highlight opportunities. *Conscientious* effort must be made to analyze (and use) meaningful information from this history, determined by answering the following:

32. Are sources of sales from market segments and their customers qualified and quantified according to size and profitability? Do you know which ones have potential for growth? _____

33. Are sales growth and profit compared and analyzed with previous plans and records? Is this information available by market, territory, and customer in your database? _____

34. Do sales and profit history show how sales break down within the product/services line? Are some products/services lagging in markets, territories, or accounts? Do you know why? Is remedial action implemented? _____

35. Are abnormal cycles or seasonalities planned for? Can they be smoothed? _____

36. Do sales and profits match previous forecasts? Have steps been taken to remedy guesstimates or faulty projections? _____

Self-examination is very important in this phase of research as the fact base for determining sales objectives. Comparing previous sales performance against comparative buying power indexes is recommended.

Sales and Marketing Management magazine's annual survey of buying power for industrial and retail markets is a good source. Their comparative indexes use metro, county, city, and state data for measurement and comparison. This demographic survey can help measure sales performance, set sales goals, and develop marketing strategies. For example, the population of Sacramento, Milwaukee, Columbus, and San Antonio are nearly the same— ranking within five places of each other. Yet they're separated by a wide margin in terms of household income, placing 73rd, 42nd, 91st, and 205th in 1996.

Use of historical sales data will provide planners with ideas of trends concerning seasonality, product profitability, geographic and customer contribution, and performance of market segments. Sales projections are also necessary to plan inventories, align territories, and provide for sales organization. Are sales in certain markets or regions worth their cost ratios? Can expenses be reduced without losing sales? Would sales in lagging places be improved if changes were made in distribution or personnel? Better answers to these and other questions can be made by studying previous history.

Competitors - Their Influence and Direction

A major responsibility of marketing is to know the competitive environment. This knowledge is essential for future planning, because marketing events likely to occur are better assessed if your competitors' actions are studied. Valuable *marketing intelligence* is gathered from auditing your competitors these following ways:

37. Who are your principal competitors, how are they positioned, and where do they seem to be headed? Are small (or new) competitors expected to come into the picture? Do we employ clipping services to monitor competitor activities? _____

38. What is known about their financial status, key personnel, facilities, product/services reputation, and pricing policies? _____

39. What are their market shares? Guesses or factual estimates? Are SEC filings for public companies examined? Are tax, Dun & Bradstreet, and Better Business Bureau reports investigated? _____

40. How do they compare in advertising, promotion, and distribution activity? Are they more or less effective? _____

41. Which user features or characteristics of their products or services stand out? _____

42. What are their greatest strengths and weaknesses? Do you exploit advantageous differences? _____

43. Is your competitive posture regarded as proactive or reactive? Are you leader or a follower? _____

It's important to identify every competitor, regardless of size. Look at their product and service, performance record, promotion activity, advertising messages, personnel, distribution, pricing, and other resources. Most of the information about them is readily available from newspaper and magazine articles, annual reports, company literature, advertising, trade shows, published statistics from trade associations, and observations from sales people and customers in the marketplace.

The basis of competition includes product, price, quality, performance, service, technological innovation, and image. The competitor's strategy can be judged by scrutinizing these elements.

Pricing - Profitability Management

Pricing controls *volume* and *profit*. There is no area of marketing activity where strategic decisions are more important. The marketing director must never be removed from pricing decisions, because they affect market position and optimum profitability. Many factors require appraisal, including the following:

44. Is current pricing policy designed to introduce, expand, or defend? Is it planned to produce profit objectives at incremental levels of volume? What is the break-even point? Has pricing policy been acceptable in the past? _____

45. Do facilities or manufacturing processes require more volume than you currently have? Does cost information reflect profit for each product, model, or service? _____

46. Are there inherent price limitations? How sensitive are profits to change in key variables of price, mix, and volume? Are underlying factors of elasticity in the demand curve considered? Is seasonality factored into production and pricing? _____

47. How does pricing compare with your competitors in similar levels of quality? _____

48. Does your key marketing staff participate in setting prices? Do they understand how pricing policy effects their own sales and profit goals? _____

49. Is your policy for deviation from established pricing policy defined and policed? _____

50. Are price lists and pricing information current, understandable, and easy to use? _____

51. Can the business support more advertising and promotion? _____

52. Do intermediates in the selling channels make enough money to motivate them? _____

53. Is the history of price deals, discounts, and promotions known? Have they produced added business justifying them? _____

54. Is pricing strategy focusing on quality of the product/services? Are key factors effecting buying decisions known? Are they emphasized in advertising and merchandising programs? _____

55. How well are your pricing strategies communicated in growth and profit plans? Are they effectively disseminated throughout the organization on a "need to know" basis? _____

Customers do not buy a product; they buy *value* represented by satisfying a want. Price may be a secondary value and only part of a range of quality considerations that are not expressed in price, such as durability, service, or delivery. Concepts of value largely depend on the service customers receive. For example, customers buy household appliances on the basis of their experience or on recommendations from friends and relatives. Speed and quality of service are major determinants in customer-preference decisions.

Noted for quality and service, Maytag's success in the home laundry market is ample testimony to this premise. Andersen's wood-framed Thermopane roll-out windows and patio doors are nationally recognized in their market niche. Product design, high quality, and good service give them widespread preference with architects, builders, and owners. Their television commercial, "Come home to Andersen," reinforces the *image of value* with both satisfied and prospective customers.

Low prices are not the only factor that made Wal-Mart the world's largest retailer. Its broad selection of merchandise, fully stocked shelves, high-tech inventory systems, and bare-bones cor-porate culture keep them from developing the big-company lethargy that infested giants such as Sears, GM, and IBM. Customers perceive Wal-Mart as a retailer that doesn't need to advertise specials because its image was built on "everyday low pricing" long before it became fashionable in the industry.

Top management must establish price policy in the context of planning marketing strategy. Is the position characterized as acquiring, defending, or expanding? Are newcomers gaining a foothold? Is position well-established, requiring defensive pricing? If pricing strategies cannot be expressed and defended, then price decisions probably reflect "me too" moves, or they're based on "rule of thumb" percentage increase. These methods almost always result in trouble. Companies should seek answers to questions such as the following:

- Will a reduced price actually generate incremental volume?

- How much incremental volume is required to offset a lower price that reduces unit profit margins?

- Are competitors likely to react in a way that will damage the overall profit structure of the business?

Symptoms of five fundamental deficiencies leading companies into pricing problems and poor profit results can be identified. First, companies often fail to understand the market in which the business operates.

- Which market segments are served and why?

- What is the relative position of each major competitor, and how do they match up on price, delivery, service, and quality?

- To what extent does market demand vary with price? What are the underlying factors that cause relative elasticity or inelasticity in the demand curve?

- How does industry capacity compare with total market demand? What significant changes in capacity are likely?

- How have industry or company pricing practices shifted in the past with changes in capacity/demand relationships?

Second, companies fail to understand the economics of the business.

- How much profit (after all allocations) is generated by each product or model?

- How does the cost and profit structure for each product vary with changes in volume?

- How many dollars of assets are committed, and what return is being earned on the investment?

- How sensitive are profits to changes in key variables of price, mix, and costs?

- What are the true idle plant costs for abandoned or unused facilities?

Third, companies fail to comprehend or act on the economics of inflation.

- Are profit returns adjusted with rates of inflation?

- Do price adjustments lag far behind increasing costs?

Fourth, companies fail to ensure that pricing policy is linked to a total marketing strategy.

- Is strategy aimed at mature, price-sensitive markets where high volume is targeted at price-oriented accounts?

- Is strategy focused on premium markets where custom design or superior performance are key factors in buying decisions?

Fifth, companies fail to maintain tight control of pricing policy.

- Does management take positive steps to explicitly follow the policy throughout the company?

- Are pricing policies defined and communicated in a set of growth and profit targets? Are they disseminated throughout the organization on a "need to know" basis?

- Does the sales force understand how pricing policy relates to achieving their own sales and profit goals?

Discretionary costs tend to be regarded as variable when volume increases and fixed when volume goes down. These discretionary costs must be scaled back to ensure cost configurations that will yield satisfactory profit margins on a lower-than-planned volume. Belt tightening is crucial when markets turn soft, and management must anticipate market conditions so that inventories, labor levels, and costs can be geared to market swings. Waiting until conditions actually reflect themselves in the profit-and-loss statement may be several months too late and may lead to panic and "jump start" reactions.

Never overlook thoughtful examination of pricing in the assessment stage of marketing planning. The marketing staff should be major players in any price-planning activity, not just bystanders to the process. Their input is indispensable, since they are the profit producers and must be privy to the pricing objectives of the business. Marketing-driven companies recognize this as part of their basic operating doctrine, but there are still some autocratic, old-school executives who rely too heavily on the financial department for all of their price decisions and policies. They still view marketing as only a selling function, failing to employ a marketing-driven and customer-oriented organizational structure. Marketing personnel must be financially literate. They should know how to read a balance sheet, an operating statement, a cash-flow statement, and understand financial ratios and other measuring sticks for evaluating company performance.

Pricing is the toughest part of marketing and the weakest link in many companies. Simply meeting competitors' pricing, increasing volume with price reductions, or getting fixed margins over cost does not maximize profit. The secret is to find the right *combination* to produce more profit from resources.

Marketing Administration
- Operational Proficiency, Customer Service, and Monetary Compensation

If a business is going to achieve its sales and profit objectives, it must have *trained* and *motivated* marketing personnel. They are your primary contacts with customers, and their performance determines, to a great degree, your business's success. There are four elements to a sale: discovering customers' needs, presenting, closing, and following through. *Poor marketers skip the first step and ignore the last!* Some important questions for appraisal (and improvement) include the following:

56. Does order processing provide for courteous, timely, and accurate handling? Are delivery dates usually kept? Are customers promptly advised of delays? _____

57. Are computer programs geared to provide meaningful data for marketing planning, implementation, and control? Does the database include account history? _____

58. How well do customers and market segments receive coverage in proportion to their potential? Are they classified according to their potential? _____

59. Are marketing costs budgeted, and effectively controlled? Are they included in the marketing plan? In balance with results? _____

60. Do bonus plans offer optimum incentive in relation to their costs? Are they designed to reward both team and individual performance? Do they include mutually predetermined objectives for each participant to achieve? _____

61. Are staff members using computer databases that make their work more productive? Do control reports go the right people in the right form and on a timely basis? _____

62. Are there deficiencies in recruitment? Is the turnover rate acceptable? Do opportunities for advancement exist? _____

63. Do training programs receive constant and factual evaluation, and are they frequently updated? Are they designed to deal with work situations relevant to employee jobs and responsibilities? Are training programs favorably regarded by the participants? Do feedback systems exist? _____

64. Are courses offered that help your employees improve their computer literacy, speaking, writing, and language proficiency? Do training and management development programs rachet upward to encourage advancement? _____

42

65. Have selling tools and communication
    with marketing personnel and accounts
    been effective? How well is everyone
    kept informed?   _____

Successful marketing programs must start with good organization of the marketing function. *Exhibit 12* in the Appendix illustrates the centralized arrangement of marketing activities. This structure creates a central head for all marketing groups, including sales and advertising. All marketing-related activities are coordinated with their appropriate impact and in their correct sequence. This centralized arrangement offers more effective results with *accountability* on the firing line for better products, better service, better pricing, better communications, and better use of resources. Customers are created and served by coordinated effort, rather than by fragmented, decentralized departments frequently working at cross-purposes with each other.

A *centralized* organization for all marketing activities requires a marketing director with more specialized skills and talents than those usually associated with a sales manager's position. In some cases, sales managers are named to become marketing directors because they are successful in their sales duties, but they may be lacking other analytical, creative, and organizational skills and experience that the marketing director's position requires.

The many duties of a marketing director are described in *Exhibit 13* in the Appendix. They are basic marketing functions, but variances will occur in their application, since marketing directors (and their personnel) do not directly manage all the mentioned duties. Direct responsibility for specifications and packaging, for example, may be vested in the engineering or product development group. Regardless, the head of marketing must work closely with everyone, because the work of other departments supports the marketing program of the company.

Choice for the top marketing position demands someone with considerable perspective, creativity, and knowledge of markets and marketing procedures. Understanding and appreciation for specialized functions of market research, pricing, selling, promotion, advertising, recruitment, and manpower development are all requisites. In short, the head of marketing must be the *quarterback* of the whole team, in charge of creating and serving customers — the key to prosperity of the business.

Customer satisfaction must be the primary objective of the marketing department, which has direct contact with users of the company's product or services. Procedures to handle orders in timely and courteous fashion are essential for achieving marketing success in today's highly competitive environment. For that matter, there can be no room for an indifferent or surly employee in any area of any company's operation, whether or not this individual has direct contact with customers. For this reason, companies who are customer-focused have strict rules and procedures for taking care of inquiries, complaints, and order follow-up to ensure satisfaction.

Effective training programs are a crucial part of human resources development that will produce long-run gains. Management must stay abreast of training needs and develop those that best fit their purposes.

Companies must also do more to improve workers' literacy. The Center for Workplace Issues and Trends, a private research firm in Horsham, Pennsylvania, in their survey with 455 respondents (nearly 80 percent), said that 65 percent needed better writing skills, but fewer than 25 percent said their firms spent training money to improve writing skills. Equally important, 59 percent reported that their workers needed more training in customer service. This disparity between training needed and what is being offered suggests that business must re-examine their budgets for workplace training, and address these deficiencies.

Sales turnover can be minimized with better selection, training, and compensation; all are critical elements of a well-run marketing program. People are the most important resource, and companies can not afford to mismanage this precious asset. Turnover should be evaluated to determine if remedial action is warranted. Compensation plans, prepared with the participation and approval of top management, are costs that should be included in marketing plan budgets.

Peter Drucker, considered an authority on the science of management, reminds managers that compensation can be a serious force in the organization. In his book, *Management — Tasks, Responsibilities, Practices*, Drucker cautions: *"All one can do to repeat, is to watch lest the compensation system reward the wrong behavior, emphasize the wrong results, and direct people away from the performance for the common good."* This is why a good compensation plan tries to incorporate objectives of good management and not just sales quotas.

The compensation plan should strive to balance individual recognition with the mission of the company. Objectives of the plan must be derived from the goals of the enterprise, and they should be spelled out in specifics that have linkage to the individual's contribution to those objectives. For marketing/sales people, this should include provision for their attainment of both sales and profit goals that are their shares of the corporate goal. Other specifics of a plan may include personal contribution to new product ideas, operating economies, suggestions for improving sales procedures, and customer development as reflected in improvement of their account base. These are tangible elements of a plan, but there are also intangible objectives for such important contributions as teamwork, cooperation, attitude, public responsibility, and personal reliability in the workplace. It is prudent not to overemphasize any single, key factor such as sales without consideration of its profitability to the business. *Balanced objectives* help to avoid "management by crisis," and they balance short-term with long-term goals of the enterprise.

The best compensation program is generally a combination of a base salary plus incentive. Some incentives may take the form of profit sharing, whereby a share of company earnings is retained and reinvested in a retirement plan. The company's contribution may be withheld or reduced if the person leaves prematurely or before normal retirement age. This provision also encourages longevity of good people, thus reducing turnover.

One popular incentive system, applicable to both large or small firms, pays an annual bonus as a percentage of the person's base salary. A percentage (frequently 20 percent of base) starts to be paid when the company achieves 80 percent of its sales and profit goal, and continues to pay one percentage point thereafter up to the percentage limit, which in this case is 20 percent. If 80 percent is the start point, it means that 100 percent is the stop point. Anything over 100 percent of the goal is arbitrarily retained for stockholders, retained earnings, etc. Some users of this plan may elect to set a start point for the bonus at 90 percent and use 110 percent as the stop point, reasoning that it offers more challenge with respect to personal achievement.

Another of the plan's advantages is that it can be provided for in budgets for the plan year, and if targets are not met, the payments are proportionate. On the scale of 20 points, a stop point or cut-off prevents paying abnormally large bonuses for what probably is a "windfall" rather than a direct result of personal performance. It is also ideally suited to sales people who receive a share of the company's sales and profit goal, linking them to the total effort of the firm.

In some variations of this plan, up to 50 percent of the person's performance bonus is discretionary, not automatic. When this variation is used, conditions for paying the discretionary share are spelled out as specific individual objectives the person is expected to achieve, above and beyond attainment of their sales and profit goal for the plan year. Discretionary objectives should always be in writing, personally discussed, and *implemented at the inception* of the plan year. Then they serve as part of a basis for an annual performance review with each person in the plan. Here is an incentive concept that attempts to avoid misdirection of management's objectives.

The best compensation plans are never perfect, but they should always reflect the objectives of the enterprise, as well as those of persons who are ultimately responsible for the achievement of its objectives. The time to evaluate marketing/sales compensation programs is during the audit phase of marketing planning. Examine strengths and weaknesses of current incentive programs to make provision for improvement.

Inventory and Delivery
- User Service Performance

Most products or services are readily available from others, and customers will turn to them when they do not get reliable service. Having the *right product* at the *right time* and at the *right place* spells marketing success. Questions that help find weak and strong points in product and service response to users include the following:

48

66. Are forecasts for production planning and inventory control regularly reviewed and adjusted with marketing personnel in a timely fashion? Are product/ service forecasts part of your marketing plan? Do they support the sales and profit plan? _____

67. Are inventories and raw materials kept in their right mix; acceptable balance? Is seasonality a factor? How is this handled in planning for inventory? _____

68. Is your inventory turnover acceptable? Comparable or better than industry standards? _____

69. Are on-line systems connected with large users to provide just-in-time delivery? _____

70. How well are delivery schedules communicated to users, and are they kept as promised? _____

71. Is the product delivered in good condition? Is shipping damage minimized? Is packaging acceptable? _____

72. Are distribution points accessible to the trade for prompt delivery and service? How well does your delivery and service compare with competition? _____

Inventory, warehousing, and transportation are physical elements of a delivery system and are vital components of any marketing program. Their specialized nature usually places them outside the direct control of marketing. However, they must never be independent or isolated, because their efficiency greatly depends on input and feedback from marketing. These arms of the tree must work harmoniously with each other in *coordinated teamwork* for a smooth-working, service-oriented response to wants and needs of the marketplace.

Order analysis is paramount to good sales administration. Customers should be classified according to their size and profitability. Product mix, generated from computer programming of incoming orders, is required for materials procurement and inventory control. Geographic and seasonal trends can be measured from sales records and identified for inventory planning and sales management. All of these elements of sales administration require effective computer programs that provide timely marketing management information. Computer programs generated from order entry analysis should provide usable data for many elements related to good marketing planning and management.

Logistics has become a hot competitive advantage as companies struggle to get the right products to the right places at the right time. In industry after industry, from cars and clothing to computers and chemicals, companies are taking this once dismal discipline off the loading dock and placing it near the top of the corporate agenda. A long and unsung activity, it has suddenly become very strategic as companies try to gain a competitive edge through their ability to deliver in timely fashion.

Last year American companies spent an estimated $670 billion, 10.5 percent of GDP, to wrap, bundle, load, unload, sort, reload, and transport goods. So clogged is the pipeline with unnecessary steps and stockpiles that the grocery industry alone believes it can take $30 billion, or nearly 10 percent of its annual operating cost out of the system. A typical box of breakfast cereal spends an estimated 104 days getting from factory to the supermarket through wholesalers, distributors, brokers, diverters, and consolidators, many of which have a warehouse.

Streamlining processes that span companies and continents isn't easy, but the payback can be enormous. In two years National Semiconductor cut its standard delivery time 47 percent, reduced distribution costs 2.5 percent, and increased sales 34 percent. They accomplished this by closing six warehouses around the globe and air-freighting its microchips to customers worldwide from a new, 125,000-square-foot distribution center in Singapore.

Saturn, whose world-class logistics system links suppliers, factories, and dealers, turns its parts inventory so fast, about 300 times a year, that it's barely there. Saturn maintains almost no inventory of components at Spring Hill, Tennessee. Instead, a central computer directs trucks to deliver pre-inspected and presorted parts at precise times to the factory's 56 receiving docks 21 hours a day, six days a week. Charged with making Saturn's network run on schedule is Ryder System, a Miami transportation services company that has become one of the largest logistics management firms in the U.S. Ryder keeps parts, people, and trucks in nearly constant motion. Tractor-pulling trailers, on average 90 percent full, arrive daily at Ryder's incoming post near the factory. There the drivers drop the trailers. Specially designed shuttle tractors then take the trailers with bar coded, reusable plastic bins full of parts and deliver them to the plant. Meanwhile, the long-haul drivers hitch their tractors to other waiting trailers stocked with empty bins to be hauled back to suppliers. Drivers insert a plastic key loaded with electronic data into an on-board computer. The screen then tells them exactly where to go, which route to take, and how much time to spend getting there.

Linked electronically to all its suppliers, Saturn automatically reorders parts each time a car rolls off the production line. This system of inventory replenishment replaces old, endlessly intricate computer programs previously used by GM to forecast future needs.

Analysts predict that the grocery industry can save $30 billion annually by streamlining logistics. At first blush, your average supermarket looks like a marvel of supply-chain efficiency. Wide aisles, fully stocked shelves, excellent variety, and many checkout lines are impressive. But behind the scenes is an industry that actually rewards companies and people for building unnecessary inventory. All along the supply-chain, sellers push discounted products onto merchandise buyers, who in turn are compensated for purchasing things cheaply even though they may sit in a warehouse for months. Now this is changing as big grocery retailers like Wal-Mart have developed electronically-controlled distribution systems. Scanners at checkout counters first appeared in 1974, and since then they have played a vital role in improving retail store efficiency. Bar codes identify the item by type, brand name, size, and flavor or color. When an order arrives, prices are assigned to products, or bar codes, in a computer connected to the checkout scanner.

The growing use of electronic messages, passing back and forth between computers, has automated and improved much of the inventory communication between suppliers and their customers. On-line systems with suppliers have implemented *just-in-time delivery*, a critical requirement in efforts to be more cost-effective in competition with domestic and foreign counterparts.

Profit-oriented marketing managers know that proper inventories and reliable deliveries are important costs, and so they must be concerned with balancing these costs against customer require- ments. Poor communication between marketing and counterparts in production, stocking, and delivery will contribute to poor performance. This dis- courages both the selling organization and their customers, who will look elsewhere for good service. Professional marketers will always give this high priority in their planning, implementing, and controlling activities.

Marketing Communications
- A Support System to Perceptualize
Product's Story

The axiom "It pays to advertise" is not always true; many variables in the marketing mix weigh into the equation to determine advertising's effectiveness. Businesses that spend the most often are not spending smart. Payback from costly outlays for *media advertising, sales promotion, publicity* and *marketing relations* must always be carefully scrutinized for their contribution to sales and profit. Commonly referred to as the *communication mix*— these components require objective evaluation and *linkage* to your marketing plan. Basic checklists for auditing these important elements in the communication mix follow:

The Marketing Communications Plan

73. Does an annual marketing communications plan exist? Is it integrated and compatible with the marketing plan? Not fragmented or unrelated? _____

74. Are all components of the communication mix managed by one person who reports to the head of marketing? _____

75. How are expenditures planned, budgeted, balanced, controlled, and evaluated for their cost-effectiveness? _____

76. Is corporate-level communication activity, apart from product/brand or service marketing, organized into a separate, but related staff? (annual reports, financial communication, community, and public relations, etc.) _____

77. Are corporate communication messages conveyed in the right format, at the right times, and in the right places? Are they linked with objectives and strategies in the marketing plan? _____

78. Does all marketing communication reflect creative and commonal messages in theme, copy, signage, slogans, literature, packaging, and other visuals for strong, consistent positioning, and user perception? _____

The first step for evaluating strengths and weaknesses of marketing communications is to examine its organizational structure in the company. Marketing-driven companies recognize that media advertising, sales promotion, publicity, and marketing relations are more successfully performed when they are aligned within the marketing department, as illustrated in *Exhibit 12* in the Appendix. Companies lacking this organization decentralize marketing activities into fragmented alignments.

Decentralized organization is typical of companies where marketing activities are segmented and placed on equal basis with each other. Advertising and sales promotion, in these situations, are not reporting directly to the head of marketing. This disjointed organization can cause start-stop, poorly targeted, mispositioned, and wasteful advertising promotion, and publicity programs. Like a winning football team, a functional marketing communications group has a competitive advantage when all of its parts work together from a well-organized marketing plan, and *directed by* **one** *quarterback* accountable for the plan.

Communications problems can stem from situations in companies where lines of responsibility are not clearly defined or understood. For whatever reason, there are cases where top management does not believe in organizational charts. Unless there is a policy against their use, charts should be included in the marketing plan, even if they are changed later on. Organizational structure is always clearer when it is diagrammed, not verbalized. "Put it in writing" is a good axiom. If the marketing plan and its functional execution cannot be described on paper, chances are pretty good that it is faulty and subject to misfire.

When feasible, and depending on company size, marketing communications programs should not be combined in the same department with corporate-level activity targeted to shareholders, employees, community, legislative, and financial investment sectors. Corporate programs generally include annual and quarterly reports to shareholders, facility brochures, corporate news releases, house organs, press kits, a speakers bureau, and financial newsletters. However, close cooperation between corporate and marketing communications groups on the divisional or subsidiary level is always essential for mutual effectiveness. For example, the shared use of artwork, logos, signage, photography, copy material, and outside production sources represent important tie-ins for better continuity, message-theme, and overall cost-effectiveness. Again, anticipating and planning the needs of both corporate and marketing programs are valuable spin-offs of a sound marketing planning process.

The first step in preparing a marketing com-munications plan is to establish a clear picture of the marketing communications mix being used. Inclusion in the marketing plan and a more detailed analysis of the activities in the plan merit a careful audit of previous success, failure, and cost-effectiveness. Which activities will be used? Were they successful in the past? How can they be improved? Should some be dropped? For the purpose of this analysis, a communication menu is shown in *Exhibit 14* in the Appendix.

Strange as it may seem to some, communications programs go astray when the distinct meanings of advertising, promotion, publicity, and marketing relations are misunderstood. The results are analogous to using a rifle for duck hunting, when a shotgun is the right weapon for the intended target. This simple analogy illustrates the importance of choosing communications tools appropriate to the situation and knowing what they are capable of doing. Advertising, promotion, publicity, and public relations are different, but related. Here is an example:

If the circus is coming to town and you paint a sign saying "Circus coming to the Fairgrounds Saturday," that's advertising.

If you put the sign on the back of an elephant and walk him into town, that's promotion.

And if the elephant walks through the Mayor's flower bed, that's publicity.

If you can get the Mayor's Ladies Garden Committee to laugh about it, that's public relations.

This anonymous analogy effectively portrays differences among communications elements used for marketing purposes. Each one serves different purposes, requiring different tools and methods of implementation, but they should be grouped together as a centralized function within the marketing department. While different, they are close cousins, requiring linkage with the objectives and strategies of the marketing plan.

Practitioners generally label advertising as "pull" strategy, employed to attract consumers, and sales promotion as "push" strategy, used to motivate sales to consumers. Because the two serve separate purposes and are different from each other, they are frequently managed by individual departments or outside agencies. To avoid working at cross-purposes that lack coordination with objectives, it becomes doubly important to manage and control their activity through the marketing communications plan, which in turn is coordinated with the marketing plan. Most companies use a combination of "pull" advertising and "push" promotion, but in the absence of good planning and implementation, it is easy for the mix to splinter and fragment.

A. Media Advertising - The Push

79. Are media objectives, strategies, tasks, and budgets integrated (and included) in the marketing plan? (logos, trademarks, TV and radio, newspaper and magazines, Web pages, direct mail, directories, catalogs, signs and billboards, telephone classifieds, etc.) _____

80. Are all forms of media explored for their cost effectiveness in the process of planning a media program (and budget) to achieve your sales goals and profit objectives? _____

81. Does the ad agency (or in-house staff) receive input from your marketing plan, so that media selection (and positioning) is linked with your marketing plan's objectives and strategies? How well is your agency (or in-house staff) kept informed? _____

82. What criteria are used to select your agency (or in-house staff) and is there objective evaluation of their performance on a regular basis? _____

83. Do frequency and size of media expenditures merit employing an in-house agency to prepare and place your media advertising? _____

84. Does research and tracking methodology objectively measure media dollars spent with marketing results? Are leads from advertising carefully followed and evaluated? What is their correlation? _____

Media advertising is a necessary tool of marketing, and its emphasis in the communication mix depends on the nature of goods or services being offered, as well as the product's *life cycle position*. Advertising is often the scapegoat and recipient for criticism, because there are so many intangibles that are difficult to measure. To evaluate media advertising, it is necessary to determine what is desired of media advertising or what purposes are to be served before planning a campaign or allocating funds. Many companies are led down blind alleys, increasing their advertising costs without carefully determining if they are getting their money's worth.

Is the objective to increase market share, to introduce a new product or service, to expand into a new market, or to grow revenues by X percent? Does it help to sell a product? Is it better to use the money for more salespeople, for training, or for some other sales support program? What is the most cost-effective media advertising mix (print, radio, television, Web page, direct mail, billboard, etc,) to employ?

All too often, advertising expenditures are based on percentages of sales, and then using this number as an index for setting budgets for next year. Actually, this is an illogical approach, a symptom of *value rigidity* and marketing *inertia*. Simply picking a number may be too little or too much. It does not mean that the advertising expenditure is correlated with marketing objectives.

Can advertising's value be definitely measured? Most executives would like to know how spending on advertising affects their product or service in the marketplace. Specifically, they want to be able to measure its profitability. An exhaustive study was developed and conducted by the Strategic Planning Institute (SPI) with support from the Ogilvy Center for Research and Development. Entitled, "How Advertising Affects Profitability and Growth for Consumer Businesses," it traced the linkage between advertising and the more general corporate results of growth and profitability. The study primarily set out to show a traceable road from advertising investment to profit payout. But in doing this, it also demonstrated that all roads to profit (including growth in market share and ability to command higher price) are linked to *perceived product quality*.

Over a period of more than 15 years (1970-1986), SPI tracked 700 consumer businesses through good and bad economic cycles in both North America and Europe. Using the Profit Impact of Market Strategy (PIMS) database, the study verifies a strong conceptual link connecting advertising to business success. Among other things, it shows that advertising is *not causal* but *associative*.

Advertising works successfully when other key marketing factors (usage, experience, pricing, distribution, and packaging) are in place.

The SPI study found that advertising is a vital ingredient to the concept of *"added value,"* which, they said, involves three interdependent components: innovation, quality, and consumer perception. Innovation without quality is short-lived; consumer perception without quality and/or innovation is only puffery; and both innovation and quality, if not translated into perceptions, may be useless because no one will know that the product is new or better.

SPI's findings follow:

- There is a relationship between perceived quality and relative price.

- Improving relative perceived quality increases market share.

- Consumer perception of quality leads to ultimate profitability of the product or service.

- Advertising influences perceived quality.

These conclusions underscored the importance of *communicating* the product's added quality or value. Marketing wisdom and business experience show that advertising must convert product data into perceptions as a component of added value, a fact that should cause top management to view advertising (and all other elements of marketing communications) as a carefully planned, up-front investment in product value, and not a variable cost.

In conclusion, it is important to remember that the intangible nature of human perceptions and allocation of resources to conceptualize "value added" will continue to require both artistic and analytical decision making. Business leaders and marketing planners need to understand that advertising, while necessary in one form or another, is only one of many essential elements in the marketing communication mix. It is not a panacea for other sales problems.

The first step in media evaluation is to be sure that media strategy fulfills the objectives outlined in the marketing plan. This presupposes that the target markets and the goals that media advertising is expected to achieve in these markets are incorporated in the marketing communications plan, which also includes the details for sales promotion, publicity, and marketing relations programs. Some typical media objectives include the following:

- Increase awareness
- Generate awareness for new product/services
- Increase brand preference
- Continue positioning--reinforcement
- Solidify customer loyalty
- Reach decision makers
- Communicate key product/service benefits
- Arrest declining trend
- Build demand for brand/product/service
- Position company as major source
- Obtain sales leads--inquiries

The second step in media evaluation is to prepare a realistic budget in the preliminary planning stages so that everyone involved knows what they have to work with. Delegate creativity to an agency (or in-house staff), but be sure they have adequate information from your marketing plan about the product, markets, competitors, and sales objectives. Refrain from acting as the art (or production) director, and concentrate on the business end of advertising activity.

Always consult with media staff in early planning stages, and not at the eleventh hour. Advance planning can be a major competitive advantage. Try to strip away any unnecessary approval layers so that the big ideas make it to the decision makers.

B. Sales Promotion - The Pull

85. Do promotions support sales objectives in your marketing plan, rather than being isolated and unrelated events? _____

86. Is provision for promotions planned (and budgeted) as part of your communications plan? _____

87. Are promotions coordinated with field selling, publicity, and media for optimum results? Are they tracked and analyzed to measure success or failure? _____

88. Have point of purchase (POP) displays been used to support special sales promotions? Do they measurably contribute to your sales campaigns? What are the reasons for success or failure? _____

89. Do merchandising incentives (contests, awards, premiums, cents-off coupons, tie-ins, samples, stuffers, and combo offers) add incremental sales that justify their cost? How is this measured? _____

90. What criteria are used for choosing trade shows? Do costs (display preparation, booth rental, staffing, travel, and promotion) produce more business and generate more goodwill? How are they scrutinized to determine their cost effectiveness? _____

It is important to understand the difference and similarities in the purposes of sales promotion and media advertising in order to properly utilize them in marketing communications programs.

Marketers usually refer to sales promotion as the "push" and media advertising as the "pull." Sometimes the meaning and purpose of these marketing communications vehicles become lost in political disputes over expenditures and shares of budgets earmarked for them. For example, direct mail and POP are considered by some marketers as media advertising, not sales promotion, because they represent printed material involving artwork and photography. Many newspaper advertisements for free coupons and lotteries are sales promotions, but advocates of media advertising may claim they are media expenditures. For purposes of planning, budget allocations, and implementation, it is necessary to properly organize, manage, and coordinate these activities being employed in the marketing communication mix.

In earlier times, sales promotion was regarded by many advertisers as an inconsequential activity used by sales departments to energize their sales programs. Media agencies viewed it as a subordinated and specialty merchandising business conducted by salesman who sold promotional items — pens, calendars, etc. — as incentives to build goodwill for the business.

But today, marketing-driven businesses recognize that sales promotion plays an effective role in stimulating the consumer's decision-making process. Psychologically, purchases are the logical result of gathering knowledge, sometimes referred to as "points of decision." Sales promotion provides the stimuli in a variety of situations: receiving direct mail in the home, seeing POP displays in a store, collecting coupons from the newspaper before going shopping, or selecting an airline for a trip because it offers "frequent flyer" bonus credit.

Plagued with "sticker shock" from escalating media costs, advertising proliferation has prompted businesses to turn to sales promotion campaigns for short-term results that can be more tangibly measured in terms of incremental sales increases. Advertisers, especially in recessionary times, are looking for "more bang for the buck." Marketers, of economic necessity, are becoming more discerning in using the myriad of choices in the communication menu, and sales promotion is taking a much more prominent position in the mix. Thus, sales promotion must be regarded as an integral part of the total marketing communication plan.

The sales promotion manager is a staff specialist who is responsible for providing promotional ideas, programs, and materials not otherwise associated with advertising or publicity functions. This position may report to the head of marketing communications, who should report to the director of marketing.

Regardless of organizational structure, sales promotion should not be divorced from advertising, sales publicity, and marketing relations. These activities are interdependent, and they must work harmoniously together to achieve objectives in the marketing plan. One cannot work effectively without the help of the other. Sales promotion is not a distant cousin invited only when management decides to energize the selling system. This knee-jerk practice leads to fragmented, poorly coordinated campaigns that frequently misfire, disrupting sales continuity rather than being a catalyst to achieve marketing goals.

Sales promotions should only be used to produce incremental business that cannot be attained through ordinary marketing activity. There is only one reason to promote a product: to increase sales relative to what they would have been if there had been no special promotion. *Strategy* should be a foremost consideration. Decide on specific actions necessary to achieve the marketing objectives. Identify the promotional device most appropriate for those actions. For example, if continuity of purchase is the objective, then promotional devices could include in-pack coupons or label-saving offers.

Promotions need to marry with other components in the marketing communications mix. Precautions are necessary to be sure the promotion is properly coordinated with other important parts of the marketing chain, not only to launch the event, but also to ensure availability of the product or service being specially promoted. For example, extra stock will be required for retailers' shelves, seats need to be available on the airline, a good selection of new autos will be required in dealers' inventories, and administrative procedures must ensure proper delivery and payment of a subscription generated from a magazine promotion.

Special promotional campaigns can bring in more business, but they can easily misfire and lose customers when their execution is not synchronized throughout the marketing system. Promotions must be preplanned, included in budgets, and tied into objectives of the marketing plan.

Successful sales promotions employ important ingredients of *creativity*, *timeliness*, *resourcefulness*, and *involvement*. These characteristics are evident in many national promotions, which can also be adopted by small companies for their local campaigns.

68

C. Publicity and Marketing Relations
- Building Goodwill

91. Is provision for publicity and marketing relations planned (and budgeted) as part of your marketing communications plan, and part of your marketing plan? Do these activities implement objectives and strategies of your marketing plan? _____

92. Are newsworthy marketing events staged and effectively publicized to generate goodwill and build awareness of your business and its products/ services? _____

93. What kinds of impressions are created about your business and its products/ services? Do they reflect a positive image? _____

94. Is business image and products/services acceptance objectively researched. Is too much credence placed on a few users' letters, some sales reports, selected key dealers' or distributors' comments? Are opinion samplings skewed to favor (or confirm) pre-conceived conclusions? _____

95. Do legislative groups and regulatory bodies and agencies for environment and safety have favorable impressions of your social responsibility and its

product/service's reputation? How are these groups reached? _____

96. Are your publicity stories about new (or improved) products or services regularly sent to trade publications, business magazines, newspapers, television, and radio? Is a special mailing list maintained for this? Are news releases followed with phone calls and visits to important publicists? _____

97. Are your sales meetings planned well in advance, budgeted, and evaluated for their value? _____

98. Is the business actively supporting community programs? Do staff members participate as extensions of goodwill? _____

99. Do representatives of distributors, dealers and accounts regularly meet with your executives to formulate marketing improvements and suggest new products/services? _____

100. Are awards given to business outlets/ locations and staff for their marketing achievement? _____

Best results are obtained when sales publicity and marketing relations are viewed by management as activities that start internally and reach outward. Practically all media consider genuinely new product stories newsworthy, and this publicity can produce many inquiries to benefit introductory marketing efforts. *New Product releases*, including glossy photos, are widely used in industry trade publications, and they generate widespread response from prospective customers and industry-related readers. The amount of publicity-originated material that finds its way into newspapers and magazines may surprise people, but it is estimated that upwards of 60 percent of the information on business pages of daily newspapers emanates from manufacturer and trade association news releases.

Press conferences are important vehicles for introducing new and innovative products. They have become a highly sophisticated method of publicizing product and service activity, which, if newsworthy, will be picked up by wire services and nationally publicized. The importance of these stories takes on a tangible value when a single story is placed with a news syndicate and appears in hundreds of newspapers across the country. The same new product story, much different in depth and detail, may appear in only a few business publications, but both have a place in a well-rounded marketing publicity program, even though one may contribute more to marketing's aims than the other.

Sales publicity is a versatile technique of marketing communications when it is used properly. It can cover markets broadly or be targeted to specific segments. Used intelligently, it can cover key publications in an industry that cannot be reached through conventional advertising or usual sales promotion. Not used frequently enough, it is an economical way to measure interest in a new product or to determine interest for a product in a new market. It can develop applications for a product that were not originally recognized by the developer. The market potential for a company using this medium is limited only by the creativity and effort put forth by the publicists.

Constructive marketing relations programs must always strive to establish good working relationships between suppliers or manufacturers and the selling channels. Like public relations, these activities do not represent paid advertisements, but they are events that gain acceptance and loyalty throughout the marketing system—salespeople, agents, distributors, dealers, and sales outlets. Good marketing relations with the trade are earned, not necessarily paid for in terms of special discounts, off-invoice allowances, or "push" money for shelf and floor space. In many respects, *productive marketing relations stem from a quality product—honestly advertised*, *fairly priced*, and *properly delivered*.

Manufacturers and suppliers must always strive for a cooperative, open relationship with their selling channels and customers. Respect and loyalty cannot be purchased like an ad in a trade journal, space on television, or time on radio. It must be earned by demonstrating fair dealing and honesty of purpose in marketing and all other business relationships. Good business ethics are absolutely essential in the marketing arena, where selling groups and customers can choose alternatives if relations and communications are counter-productive. Far too many companies, often unknowingly, create adversarial and confrontational situations in their day-to-day marketing programs that also require participatory programs with the selling channels. Dealer and distributor councils, sales meetings, and involvement in trade association conferences are useful and constructive vehicles for building better marketing relations with the trade.

Recognition awards and *testimonials* for service and performance are always productive parts of a well-rounded marketing relations mix, and they should be publicized in trade journals and the recipients' local newspaper and radio as part of an ongoing marketing relations program. By comparison with advertising and sales promotion, these expenditures are minuscule, and the results can be invaluable when measured in terms of goodwill and loyalty. They can be priceless commodities in a fierce, dog-eat-dog, competitive environment.

In summary, and in reference to the importance of marketing relations and publicity, executives and business owners must always be mindful that marketing produces *profit*. Product research and development, engineering and manufacturing, accounting, and human resources are necessary cost centers until marketing produces sales to support the costs of doing business and returning profits to shareholders. Therefore, conscientious efforts must always be focused on building *mutually productive* marketing relations with the selling system and the customers, who in the final analysis, create and perpetuate the business.

APPENDIX

Exhibit 1

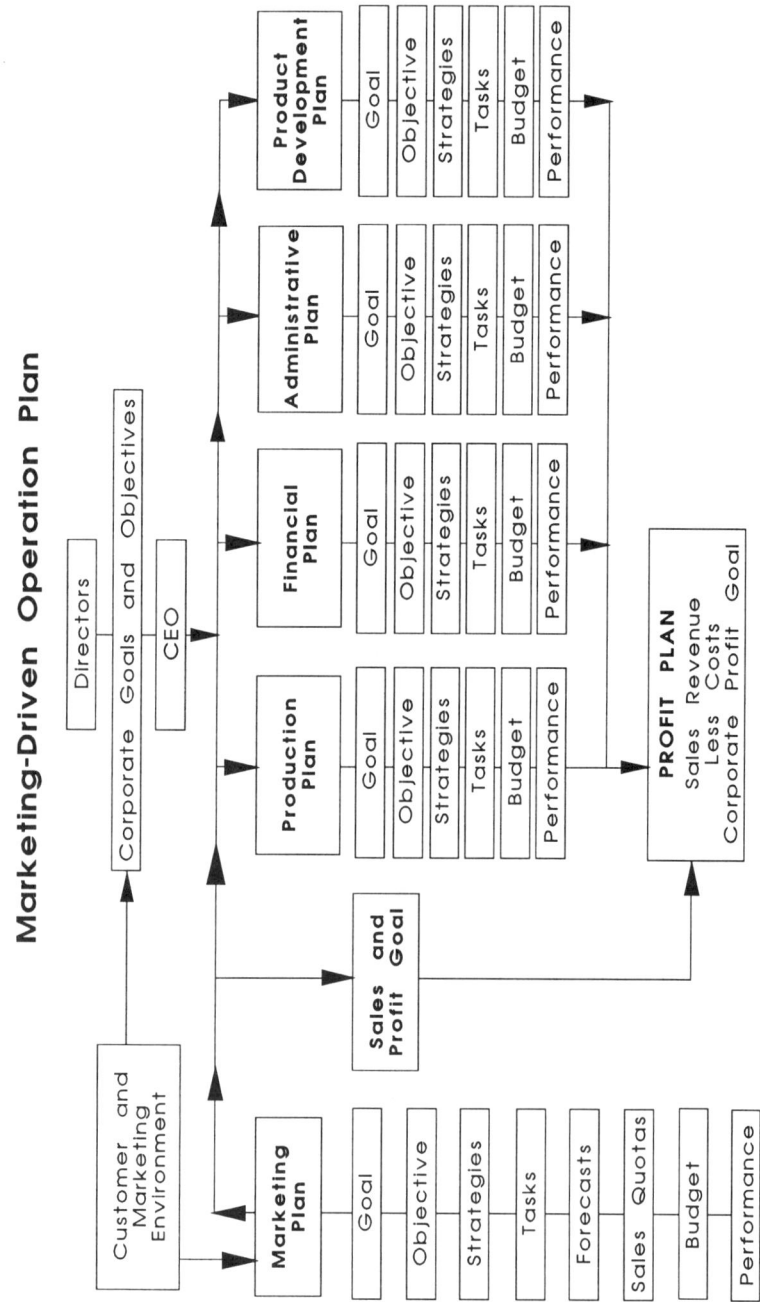

Exhibit 2

The Marketing Planning Process: EPIC©

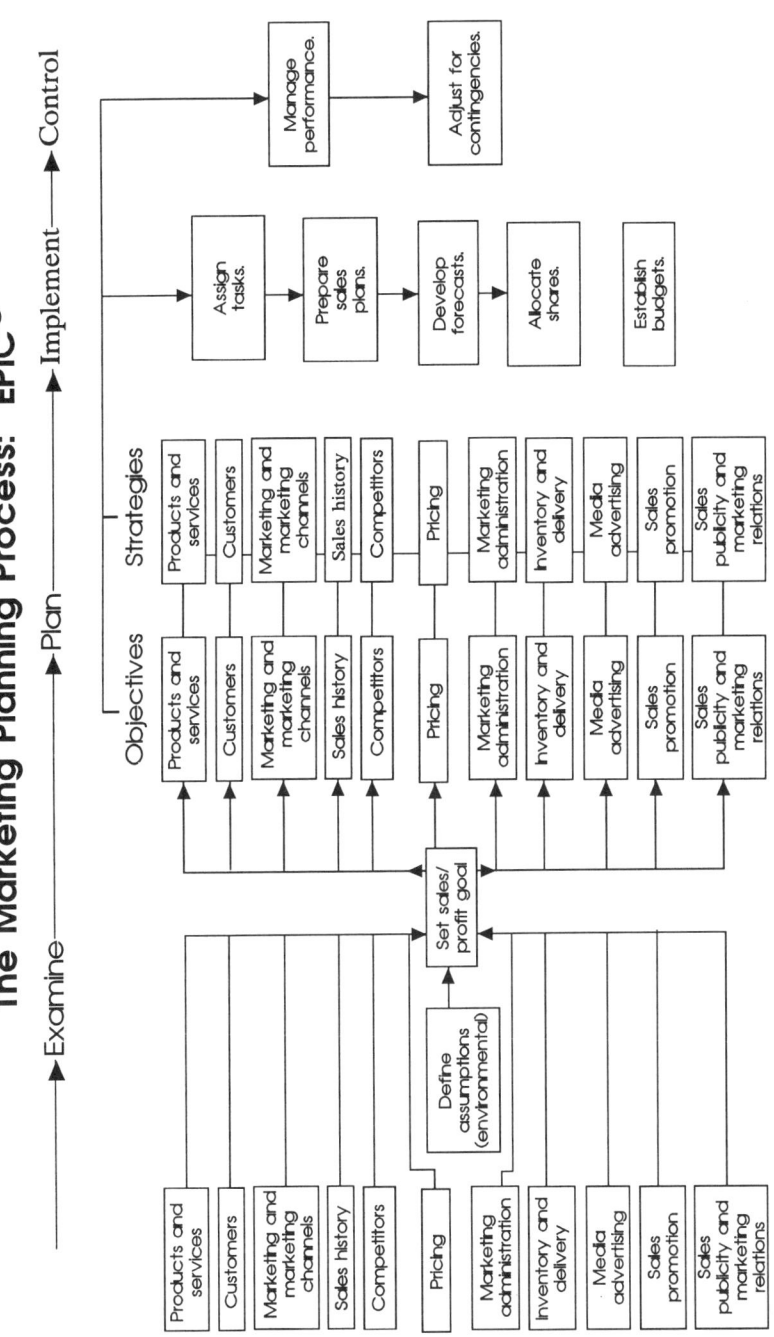

Relationships of Marketing Planning Goals, Objectives, Strategies, and Tasks

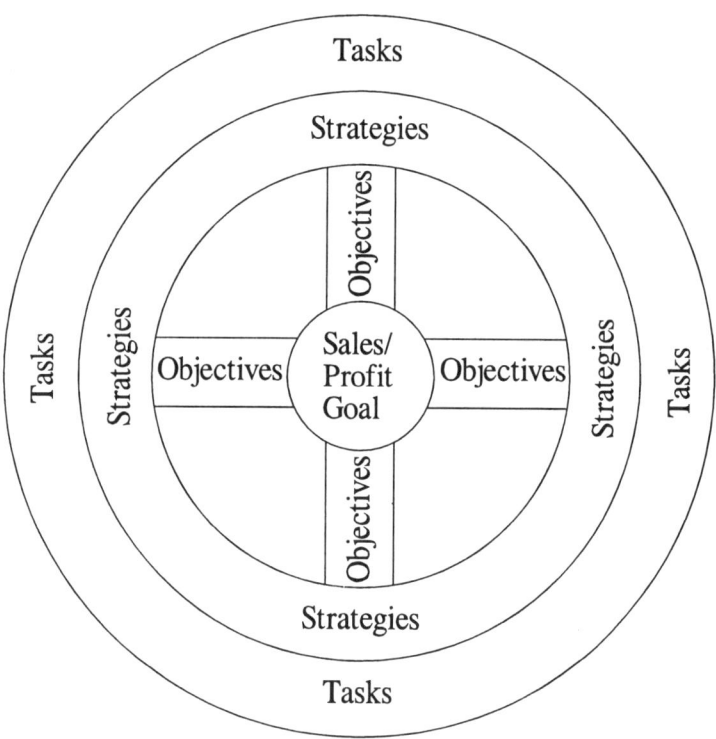

Exhibit 4

Benefits of Marketing Plans

- The marketing audit, on which all planning is based, allows self-examination, which uncovers strengths and weaknesses. Strengths can be exploited and weaknesses can be compensated. Systematic identification of opportunity is a by-product of the examination process.

- Planning produces innovation necessary for future growth. New ideas are generated. New approaches to the marketplace and its needs result from good marketing planning.

- Resources are used more efficiently because marketing operations are coordinated around selected objectives. This clarifies priorities and focuses on key elements in the marketing mix. Costs are reduced with increased spans of control.

- Better organization and accountability are created with assignment of responsibility throughout levels of managerial structure. Individuals on many levels assume responsibility for risks of business as they participate in the planning process. Deadlines are set for accomplishment. MBO is practiced.

- Planning stimulates the future in a problem-solving manner and foresees threats. Thus, earlier decisions can be made in terms of their probable impact on future activity. Crisis and change that may occur after the plan is put into motion can be more easily dealt with, because alternatives have already been explored in the process of preparing the plan.

- Budgeting is more realistic, because costs are evaluated in advance of expenditure, as part of the plan's support system and not as a separate control function of the finance department.

- As a communication tool, marketing planning encourages more participation on all levels. It promotes thinking in terms of end results as it anticipates problems and provides for contingencies. Group participation minimizes conflict and ambiguity. A team spirit in which all participants are part of the decision-making process is conducive to better morale and productivity.

- Formal marketing plans will aid in obtaining, and retaining avenues of financing. Today, most financial institutions require business and marketing plans as a prerequisite for loans.

Exhibit 5

Marketing Planning Pitfalls

- Assuming that top management can delegate the planning function to a planner.
- Failing to spend sufficient time on marketing planning or starting late
- Failing to develop suitable and realistic corporate profit goals as a basis for formulating marketing plans.
- CEO and top-level management's failure to assume necessary involvement in the process; giving it lip service.
- Failing to use plans as standards for measuring managerial performance.
- CEO's failure to create a climate in the organization that is open to planning.
- Assuming that marketing planning is something apart from the entire management process, something the marketing department does.
- Failing to hold regular reviews between top management and departmental or divisional heads regarding plans.
- Top management's making intuitive decisions that conflict with (or override) plans.
- Trying to do too much in an inadequate amount of time.
- Assuming that the plan is a blueprint that cannot be changed until the next planning cycle; not adjusting plan to unforeseen events in time.
- Ignoring line managers throughout the organization in the planning process.
- Premature and wishful expectations that the marketing plan will solve all marketing problems.
- Centralizing the planning process without enough involvement from divisions or operating units; include key staff from all areas of the organization.
- Failing to recognize or exploit planning as a management tool that can improve management capabilities.

Marketing plans are not mandates; they are *direction*. They are *not* commands; they are *commitments*.

Calendar for Marketing Planning

EPIC© _Examine_ - _Plan_ - _Implement_ - _Control_

Date	Event	Activity
Week 1	Opening Planning Meeting	CEO and key staff outline goals and planning guidelines in general session.
Weeks 1-6	**Examine**	Perform marketing audit; including previous sales history, markets, products, marketing channels, pricing, competition, advertising, promotion, publicity and marketing relations, staffing, training, and all other marketing activities.
Weeks 7-11	**Plan**	Define planning assumptions, set sales and profit goals, establish marketing objectives, and prepare strategies to attain the objectives.
Week 11	General Review Meeting	Review assumptions, goals, objectives, and their strategies for adequacy and feasibility.
Weeks 12-16	**Implement** (Preparation)	Assign planning tasks and prepare marketing budgets, to include product and sales forecasts with budgets for staffing, advertising, promotion, and marketing relations.
Week 17	Approval Meeting	Evaluate final plan with participation of key participants.
Weeks 18-20	**Implement** (Transmittal)	Make final adjustments and issue plans to all "need to know" employees.
Week 20	**Implement** (Inception)	Launch plan ahead of fiscal year.
Week 20 onward	**Control**	Conduct monthly staff meetings to measure progress and adjust plan as conditions warrant throughout plan year.

Exhibit 7

Criteria for a Good Marketing Plan

Timely   promptly implemented at start of
                the fiscal period, not yesterday's
                old milk.

Understandable well organized and understand-
                able — readable

Complete   includes ALL components of
                marketing activity, both internal
                and external

Specific   pinpoints goals: determine
                objectives, strategies, and tasks to
                achieve them with accountability
                for their completion; who, what,
                when, and where, including
                expense budgets.

Adaptable   responds to external and internal
                marketing environment and is
                compatible with corporate goals
                and company's resources.

Flexible   adjusts to changing market con-
                ditions as unforeseen events
                require alterations.

Exhibit 8

Guidelines For Making
People More Agreeable To Change

- Change is more acceptable when it is understood than when it is not.

- Change is more acceptable when it does not threaten security than when it does.

- Change is more acceptable when those affected have helped to create it than when it has been externally imposed.

- Change is more acceptable when it results from an application of previously established impersonal principles than when it is dictated by personal order.

- Change is more acceptable when it follows a series of successful changes than when it follows a series of failures.

- Change is more acceptable when it is inaugurated after prior change has been assimilated than when it is inaugurated during confusion or other major changes.

- Change is more acceptable to people who share in the benefits than to those who do not.

- Change is more acceptable to people new on a job than to people already established in a job.

- Change is more acceptable to people if it is planned than if it is haphazard.

- Change is more acceptable if the organization has been trained to plan for improvement than if the organization is accustomed to static procedures.

George A. Steiner, *Strategic Planning* (New York: The Free Press, a division of Macmillan, Inc., 1979).

Exhibit 9

New Product/Service
Screening and Development

Financial

- What is the anticipated return on investment?
- What is the payback period?
- Where is the break-even point?
- Is start-up capital available?

Legal

- Is the product/service patentable?
- Are there federal, state, or local restrictions?
- Is the product/service offensive to environments in which it will be used?
- How significant are warranty or service problems?

Potential Market and Marketing Compatibility

- What is the market's size and how is it segmented?
- Where is the primary market located?
- Is the need for the product differentiated or undifferentiated?
- How fast can the market/s grow?
- Is this product/service innovative, and what does it replace?
- Who are the likely competitors, and what are their strengths and weaknesses?
- Is profitability attractive enough to support marketing costs?
- Can the selling system absorb the product/service, or does it require separate and/or additional sales power?

Engineering and Production

- Is the product/service technically feasible?
- Can it be produced at a marketable cost-profit ratio?
- Is there production capability, including storage facility for materials and finished products/services?
- Will special machinery or equipment be required?
- Are timetables for prototypes, pilot production, and full-scale production established?

Exhibit 10

Characteristics of Product Life Cycle Stages

Stage	Nature of Market	Profitability
Introduction	Innovative exclusivity Gradual sales growth Undifferentiated demand Awareness advertising Pricing latitude	Marginal-Good
Growth	Minimal competition Imitators Rapid sales increase Widespread demand Undifferentiated Preference advertising Selective price adjustments	Excellent
Maturity	Strong competition, niches Slowing sales increase Differentiated demand Segmentation Brand loyalty advertising Price sensitivity, softening	Good
Saturation	Competitive proliferation Sales plateau Declining markets Reinforcement advertising Pruning and diversification Downward price pressure	Fair
Decline	New innovators Old competitors Decreasing sales Fewer markets Belt tightening Cost reductions Reminder advertising Price deterioration	Poor

Exhibit 11

Product Matrixation

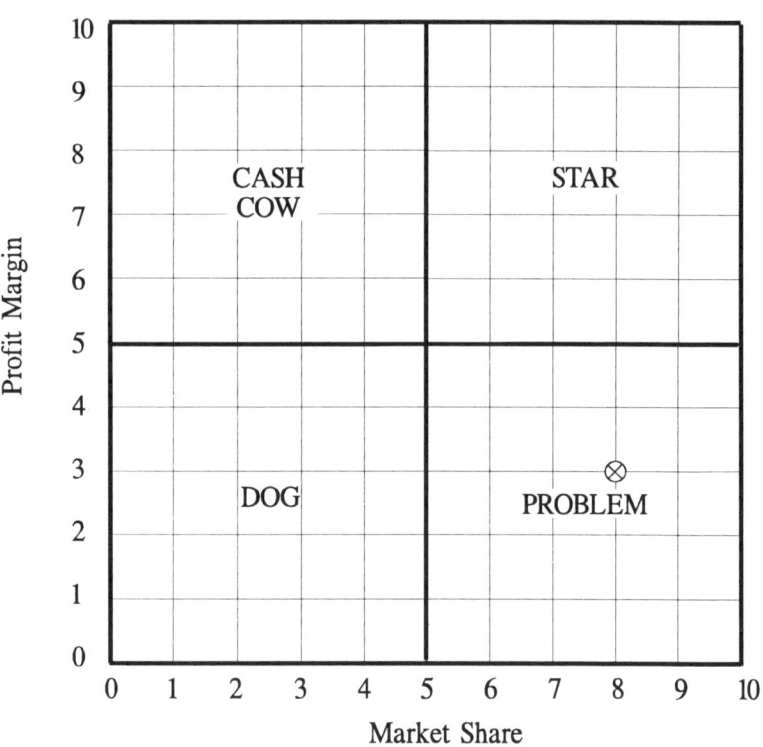

Market Share

Exhibit 12

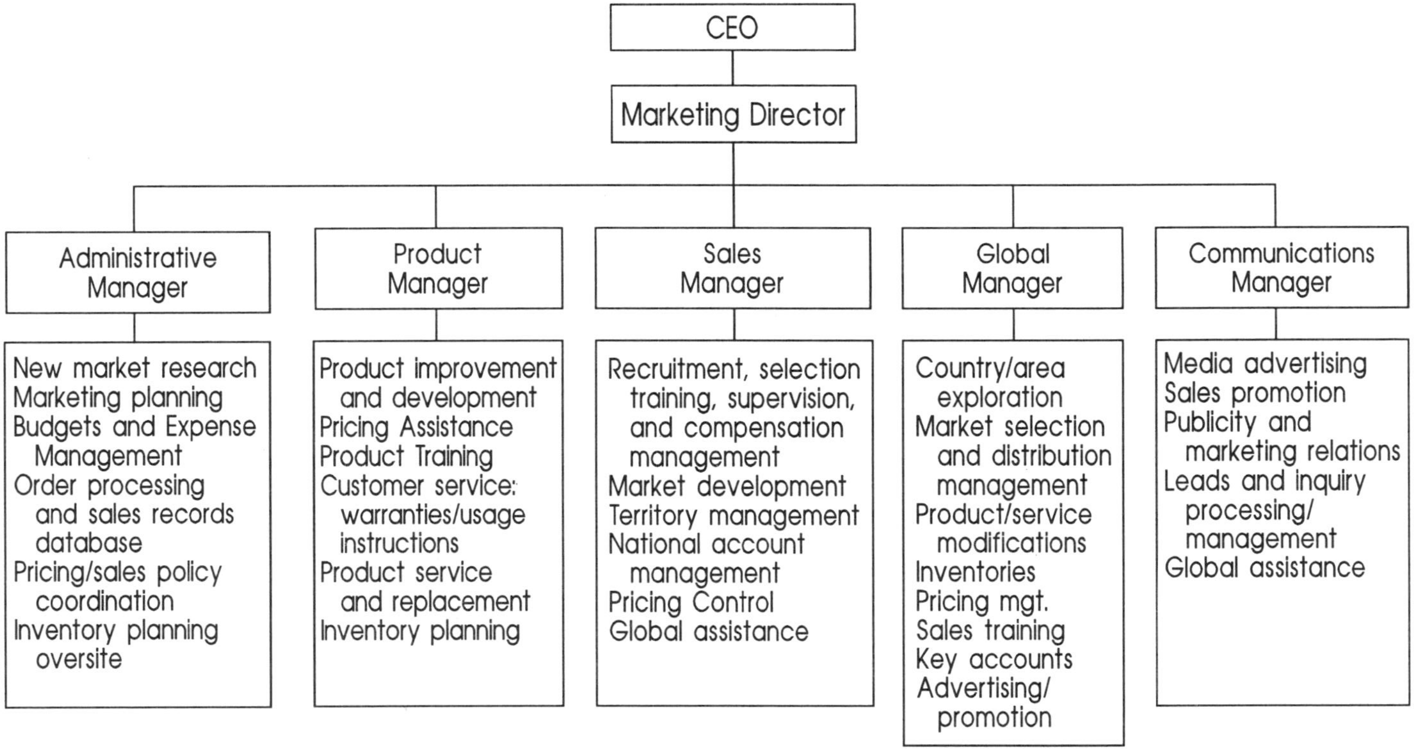

```
                                    CEO
                                     |
                            Marketing Director
                                     |
   ┌──────────────┬──────────────┬───┴──────────┬──────────────┬──────────────┐
Administrative   Product        Sales          Global         Communications
Manager          Manager        Manager        Manager        Manager
```

Administrative Manager	Product Manager	Sales Manager	Global Manager	Communications Manager
New market research	Product improvement and development	Recruitment, selection training, supervision, and compensation management	Country/area exploration	Media advertising
Marketing planning	Pricing Assistance	Market development	Market selection and distribution management	Sales promotion
Budgets and Expense Management	Product Training	Territory management	Product/service modifications	Publicity and marketing relations
Order processing and sales records database	Customer service: warranties/usage instructions	National account management	Inventories	Leads and inquiry processing/ management
Pricing/sales policy coordination	Product service and replacement	Pricing Control	Pricing mgt.	Global assistance
Inventory planning oversite	Inventory planning	Global assistance	Sales training	
			Key accounts	
			Advertising/ promotion	

Exhibit 13

Marketing Director Position Description

- Manage preparation of the annual marketing plan.

- Identify markets for present and new products.

- Manage channels of distribution delivering products/services at the right times and right places.

- Measure position (market shares) in markets being served.

- Recommend new products/services, prune existing ones, and search for user needs and wants that exist or can be created.

- Assure provision (through customer service channels) for usage instructions, maintenance, and replacement service.

- Forecast sales in units and dollars on monthly basis for production and cash planning.

- Coordinate marketing mix programs motivating purchase, including sales, advertising, promotion, publicity, and marketing relations.

- Implement sales policies/procedures and monitor sales performance against the marketing plan.

- Manage sales expense budgets; allocate shares (according to markets, representation, etc.) supporting the forecast.

- Implement pricing policies for optimum profitability.

- Oversee selection, training, management, and compensation of personnel in the marketing department, including budgets.

- Monitor order processing.

- Assist with credit and collection procedures.

- Oversee preparation of specifications, packaging, branding, and sales literature.

Exhibit 14

Marketing Communication Mix

Media Advertising

Print
  Newspapers
  Consumer magazines
  Trade publications
  Industry directories
  Signs and billboards
  Telephone, classifieds
  Direct mail and stuffers
  Logos and trademarks
  Web pages

Television
  Network, syndicated
  Cable
  Local and national spot

Radio (AM and FM)

Sales Promotion

Sales literature, catalogs
Merchandising incentives
  Premiums
  Cents-off and rebate
    coupons
  Gratuities
  Samplings
  Merchandise tie-ins
  Contests and lotteries
Co-op advertising, market
  building
Promotional teleselling
Research telemarketing
POP displays
Trade shows and exhibits
Audio-visual programs
Samples and demos

Publicity and Marketing Relations

Consumer and trade relations
Sales, product, and people recognition awards
Trade newsletters and bulletins
News releases and press conferences
Sales conferences, meetings, and trade shows
Clipping services
Archives and museums

Exhibit 15

Checklist for Marketing Plan Control

1. Start early! Formal planning activity should begin no later than early September if the plan period starts on January 1. (Allow approximately 20 weeks before fiscal period begins.)

2. Schedule regular meetings to review planning progress. Be sure to include key people throughout the organization who are instrumental in the plan's implementation. They will be more motivated to execute it if they are part of the planning process.

3. Do not take shortcuts! Get facts, not guessimates.

4. Always be specific and thorough.

5. Prepare timetables with assignments and deadlines for their completion.

6. Communicate plans through all appropriate channels on a need-to-know basis before fiscal period starts.

7. Hold regular progress meetings after the plan is in motion, generally on a monthly basis.

8. Adjust the plan when marketing conditions warrant change.

9. Do not let formality replace originality. The KISS (Keep It Simple, Sam) acronym is still important to the result!

10. **Be ever-mindful that the greatest problem in communication is the illusion that it has been achieved.**

Exhibit 16

The Four EPIC© Steps to
Effective Marketing Planning

1. Examine

Perform a careful analysis of the marketplace environment and your marketing power within it. A thorough and complete audit will provide insight into performance, pointing to strengths and weaknesses that must be addressed in marketing planning.

Examination must include all *external* factors such as markets, competition, government regulation, funding sources, and general economic outlook. *Internal* components of the marketing mix, such as corporate marketing culture, products/services, customers, marketing channels, order process, marketing history and sales records, pricing, marketing administration, and staffing to include recruitment, training, and compensation. Also include marketing communications that incorporate advertising, promotion, publicity, and public relations must be evaluated.

2. Plan

Set the financial and operating goals after examining your operating environment in Step 1. Briefly explain the assumptions being used to arrive at the goals.

Prepare clear and focused *objectives* to achieve your operating goals, together with specific strategies and tasks, achieve these objectives. All areas of the marketing mix enumerated in Step 1 should be addressed in Step 2.

3. Implement

Plans must never become ends unto themselves. They are nothing without execution. Implement the planning process and convert objectives, their strategies, and their tasks into action!

This step requires completing "how-to" tasks necessary to fulfill supporting strategies, and their objectives established in Step 2.

Product forecasts should be included.

Tasks required to accomplish everything (with control schedules) include allocating marketing costs with breakdowns of expenditures to achieve them. Expense budgets (with their time frames) for media advertising, promotion, marketing relations and publicity, staffing, and all other marketing costs must be prepared and included.

4. **Control**

Use a performance review system that measures progress against plan, as shown in *Exhibit 17*, page 92. Meet at regular intervals (usually monthly) with appropriate top management to discuss its effectiveness. Adjust the plan to changes in the environment as they occur.

Remember that all plans are imperfect, because they cannot predict events with certainty. *Be prepared to adjust for unexpected circumstances.*

Monthly Marketing Plan Performance Report

	Plan $	Actual $	Variance %	YTD Variance %
Sales (total dollars)				
Units				
Product				
Territory				
Customer				
Profit (gross)				
Product				
Territory				
Customer				
Total Marketing Expense				
Administrative staff				
Field sales staff				
Clerical staff				
Training and development				
Customer service				
Travel				
Media advertising				
Sales promotion				
Marketing relations and publicity				
Supplies and equipment				
Rent and utilities				
Miscellaneous				

The Business Marketing Association is a not-for-profit continuing education resource for business-to-business marketers. BMA offers a wide range of professional development materials and programs, including job referral, conferences, seminars, videos, CD's, newsletters, books, studies, white papers, a communications award competition and a certification credential.

BMA's website, *www.marketing,org*, provides a connection to members throughout the world. For more information, call 1-800-644-4BMA, or email *bma@marketing.org*.